C-1145 CAREER EXAMINATION SERIES

THIS IS YOUR **PASSBOOK**® FOR ...

BUILDING CONSTRUCTION ESTIMATOR

NATIONAL LEARNING CORPORATION®
passbooks.com

COPYRIGHT NOTICE

This book is SOLELY intended for, is sold ONLY to, and its use is RESTRICTED to individual, bona fide applicants or candidates who qualify by virtue of having seriously filed applications for appropriate license, certificate, professional and/or promotional advancement, higher school matriculation, scholarship, or other legitimate requirements of educational and/or governmental authorities.

This book is NOT intended for use, class instruction, tutoring, training, duplication, copying, reprinting, excerption, or adaptation, etc., by:

1) Other publishers
2) Proprietors and/or Instructors of «Coaching» and/or Preparatory Courses
3) Personnel and/or Training Divisions of commercial, industrial, and governmental organizations
4) Schools, colleges, or universities and/or their departments and staffs, including teachers and other personnel
5) Testing Agencies or Bureaus
6) Study groups which seek by the purchase of a single volume to copy and/or duplicate and/or adapt this material for use by the group as a whole without having purchased individual volumes for each of the members of the group
7) Et al.

Such persons would be in violation of appropriate Federal and State statutes.

PROVISION OF LICENSING AGREEMENTS. — Recognized educational, commercial, industrial, and governmental institutions and organizations, and others legitimately engaged in educational pursuits, including training, testing, and measurement activities, may address request for a licensing agreement to the copyright owners, who will determine whether, and under what conditions, including fees and charges, the materials in this book may be used them. In other words, a licensing facility exists for the legitimate use of the material in this book on other than an individual basis. However, it is asseverated and affirmed here that the material in this book CANNOT be used without the receipt of the express permission of such a licensing agreement from the Publishers. Inquiries re licensing should be addressed to the company, attention rights and permissions department.

All rights reserved, including the right of reproduction in whole or in part, in any form or by any means, electronic or mechanical, including photocopying, recording, or by any information storage and retrieval system, without permission in writing from the Publisher.

Copyright © 2020 by

NLC®

National Learning Corporation

212 Michael Drive, Syosset, NY 11791
(516) 921-8888 • www.passbooks.com
E-mail: info@passbooks.com

PUBLISHED IN THE UNITED STATES OF AMERICA

PASSBOOK® SERIES

THE *PASSBOOK® SERIES* has been created to prepare applicants and candidates for the ultimate academic battlefield – the examination room.

At some time in our lives, each and every one of us may be required to take an examination – for validation, matriculation, admission, qualification, registration, certification, or licensure.

Based on the assumption that every applicant or candidate has met the basic formal educational standards, has taken the required number of courses, and read the necessary texts, the *PASSBOOK® SERIES* furnishes the one special preparation which may assure passing with confidence, instead of failing with insecurity. Examination questions – together with answers – are furnished as the basic vehicle for study so that the mysteries of the examination and its compounding difficulties may be eliminated or diminished by a sure method.

This book is meant to help you pass your examination provided that you qualify and are serious in your objective.

The entire field is reviewed through the huge store of content information which is succinctly presented through a provocative and challenging approach – the question-and-answer method.

A climate of success is established by furnishing the correct answers at the end of each test.

You soon learn to recognize types of questions, forms of questions, and patterns of questioning. You may even begin to anticipate expected outcomes.

You perceive that many questions are repeated or adapted so that you can gain acute insights, which may enable you to score many sure points.

You learn how to confront new questions, or types of questions, and to attack them confidently and work out the correct answers.

You note objectives and emphases, and recognize pitfalls and dangers, so that you may make positive educational adjustments.

Moreover, you are kept fully informed in relation to new concepts, methods, practices, and directions in the field.

You discover that you arre actually taking the examination all the time: you are preparing for the examination by "taking" an examination, not by reading extraneous and/or supererogatory textbooks.

In short, this PASSBOOK®, used directedly, should be an important factor in helping you to pass your test.

BUILDING CONSTRUCTION ESTIMATOR

DUTIES:

Performs highly technical estimating work in determining the quantities and costs of materials used for construction or alterations of government owned or leased buildings; performs related duties as required.

SUBJECT OF EXAMINATION:

The written test designed to evaluate knowledge, skills and /or abilities in the following areas:

1. Principles and practices of building construction;
2. Drawings, specifications and contract documents;
3. Building construction quantity and cost estimates;
4. Mechanical and electrical systems in buildings issues; and
5. Understanding and interpreting written material.

HOW TO TAKE A TEST

I. YOU MUST PASS AN EXAMINATION

A. WHAT EVERY CANDIDATE SHOULD KNOW

Examination applicants often ask us for help in preparing for the written test. What can I study in advance? What kinds of questions will be asked? How will the test be given? How will the papers be graded?

As an applicant for a civil service examination, you may be wondering about some of these things. Our purpose here is to suggest effective methods of advance study and to describe civil service examinations.

Your chances for success on this examination can be increased if you know how to prepare. Those "pre-examination jitters" can be reduced if you know what to expect. You can even experience an adventure in good citizenship if you know why civil service exams are given.

B. WHY ARE CIVIL SERVICE EXAMINATIONS GIVEN?

Civil service examinations are important to you in two ways. As a citizen, you want public jobs filled by employees who know how to do their work. As a job seeker, you want a fair chance to compete for that job on an equal footing with other candidates. The best-known means of accomplishing this two-fold goal is the competitive examination.

Exams are widely publicized throughout the nation. They may be administered for jobs in federal, state, city, municipal, town or village governments or agencies.

Any citizen may apply, with some limitations, such as the age or residence of applicants. Your experience and education may be reviewed to see whether you meet the requirements for the particular examination. When these requirements exist, they are reasonable and applied consistently to all applicants. Thus, a competitive examination may cause you some uneasiness now, but it is your privilege and safeguard.

C. HOW ARE CIVIL SERVICE EXAMS DEVELOPED?

Examinations are carefully written by trained technicians who are specialists in the field known as "psychological measurement," in consultation with recognized authorities in the field of work that the test will cover. These experts recommend the subject matter areas or skills to be tested; only those knowledges or skills important to your success on the job are included. The most reliable books and source materials available are used as references. Together, the experts and technicians judge the difficulty level of the questions.

Test technicians know how to phrase questions so that the problem is clearly stated. Their ethics do not permit "trick" or "catch" questions. Questions may have been tried out on sample groups, or subjected to statistical analysis, to determine their usefulness.

Written tests are often used in combination with performance tests, ratings of training and experience, and oral interviews. All of these measures combine to form the best-known means of finding the right person for the right job.

II. HOW TO PASS THE WRITTEN TEST

A. NATURE OF THE EXAMINATION

To prepare intelligently for civil service examinations, you should know how they differ from school examinations you have taken. In school you were assigned certain definite pages to read or subjects to cover. The examination questions were quite detailed and usually emphasized memory. Civil service exams, on the other hand, try to discover your present ability to perform the duties of a position, plus your potentiality to learn these duties. In other words, a civil service exam attempts to predict how successful you will be. Questions cover such a broad area that they cannot be as minute and detailed as school exam questions.

In the public service similar kinds of work, or positions, are grouped together in one "class." This process is known as *position-classification*. All the positions in a class are paid according to the salary range for that class. One class title covers all of these positions, and they are all tested by the same examination.

B. FOUR BASIC STEPS

1) Study the announcement

How, then, can you know what subjects to study? Our best answer is: "Learn as much as possible about the class of positions for which you've applied." The exam will test the knowledge, skills and abilities needed to do the work.

Your most valuable source of information about the position you want is the official exam announcement. This announcement lists the training and experience qualifications. Check these standards and apply only if you come reasonably close to meeting them.

The brief description of the position in the examination announcement offers some clues to the subjects which will be tested. Think about the job itself. Review the duties in your mind. Can you perform them, or are there some in which you are rusty? Fill in the blank spots in your preparation.

Many jurisdictions preview the written test in the exam announcement by including a section called "Knowledge and Abilities Required," "Scope of the Examination," or some similar heading. Here you will find out specifically what fields will be tested.

2) Review your own background

Once you learn in general what the position is all about, and what you need to know to do the work, ask yourself which subjects you already know fairly well and which need improvement. You may wonder whether to concentrate on improving your strong areas or on building some background in your fields of weakness. When the announcement has specified "some knowledge" or "considerable knowledge," or has used adjectives like "beginning principles of..." or "advanced ... methods," you can get a clue as to the number and difficulty of questions to be asked in any given field. More questions, and hence broader coverage, would be included for those subjects which are more important in the work. Now weigh your strengths and weaknesses against the job requirements and prepare accordingly.

3) Determine the level of the position

Another way to tell how intensively you should prepare is to understand the level of the job for which you are applying. Is it the entering level? In other words, is this the position in which beginners in a field of work are hired? Or is it an intermediate or advanced level? Sometimes this is indicated by such words as "Junior" or "Senior" in the class title. Other jurisdictions use Roman numerals to designate the level – Clerk I, Clerk II, for example. The word "Supervisor" sometimes appears in the title. If the level is not indicated by the title, check the description of duties. Will you be working under very close supervision, or will you have responsibility for independent decisions in this work?

4) Choose appropriate study materials

Now that you know the subjects to be examined and the relative amount of each subject to be covered, you can choose suitable study materials. For beginning level jobs, or even advanced ones, if you have a pronounced weakness in some aspect of your training, read a modern, standard textbook in that field. Be sure it is up to date and has general coverage. Such books are normally available at your library, and the librarian will be glad to help you locate one. For entry-level positions, questions of appropriate difficulty are chosen – neither highly advanced questions, nor those too simple. Such questions require careful thought but not advanced training.

If the position for which you are applying is technical or advanced, you will read more advanced, specialized material. If you are already familiar with the basic principles of your field, elementary textbooks would waste your time. Concentrate on advanced textbooks and technical periodicals. Think through the concepts and review difficult problems in your field.

These are all general sources. You can get more ideas on your own initiative, following these leads. For example, training manuals and publications of the government agency which employs workers in your field can be useful, particularly for technical and professional positions. A letter or visit to the government department involved may result in more specific study suggestions, and certainly will provide you with a more definite idea of the exact nature of the position you are seeking.

III. KINDS OF TESTS

Tests are used for purposes other than measuring knowledge and ability to perform specified duties. For some positions, it is equally important to test ability to make adjustments to new situations or to profit from training. In others, basic mental abilities not dependent on information are essential. Questions which test these things may not appear as pertinent to the duties of the position as those which test for knowledge and information. Yet they are often highly important parts of a fair examination. For very general questions, it is almost impossible to help you direct your study efforts. What we can do is to point out some of the more common of these general abilities needed in public service positions and describe some typical questions.

1) General information

Broad, general information has been found useful for predicting job success in some kinds of work. This is tested in a variety of ways, from vocabulary lists to questions about current events. Basic background in some field of work, such as sociology or economics, may be sampled in a group of questions. Often these are principles which have become familiar to most persons through exposure rather than through formal training. It is difficult to advise you how to study for these questions; being alert to the world around you is our best suggestion.

2) Verbal ability

An example of an ability needed in many positions is verbal or language ability. Verbal ability is, in brief, the ability to use and understand words. Vocabulary and grammar tests are typical measures of this ability. Reading comprehension or paragraph interpretation questions are common in many kinds of civil service tests. You are given a paragraph of written material and asked to find its central meaning.

3) Numerical ability

Number skills can be tested by the familiar arithmetic problem, by checking paired lists of numbers to see which are alike and which are different, or by interpreting charts and graphs. In the latter test, a graph may be printed in the test booklet which you are asked to use as the basis for answering questions.

4) Observation

A popular test for law-enforcement positions is the observation test. A picture is shown to you for several minutes, then taken away. Questions about the picture test your ability to observe both details and larger elements.

5) Following directions

In many positions in the public service, the employee must be able to carry out written instructions dependably and accurately. You may be given a chart with several columns, each column listing a variety of information. The questions require you to carry out directions involving the information given in the chart.

6) Skills and aptitudes

Performance tests effectively measure some manual skills and aptitudes. When the skill is one in which you are trained, such as typing or shorthand, you can practice. These tests are often very much like those given in business school or high school courses. For many of the other skills and aptitudes, however, no short-time preparation can be made. Skills and abilities natural to you or that you have developed throughout your lifetime are being tested.

Many of the general questions just described provide all the data needed to answer the questions and ask you to use your reasoning ability to find the answers. Your best preparation for these tests, as well as for tests of facts and ideas, is to be at your physical and mental best. You, no doubt, have your own methods of getting into an exam-taking mood and keeping "in shape." The next section lists some ideas on this subject.

IV. KINDS OF QUESTIONS

Only rarely is the "essay" question, which you answer in narrative form, used in civil service tests. Civil service tests are usually of the short-answer type. Full instructions for answering these questions will be given to you at the examination. But in case this is your first experience with short-answer questions and separate answer sheets, here is what you need to know:

1) Multiple-choice Questions

Most popular of the short-answer questions is the "multiple choice" or "best answer" question. It can be used, for example, to test for factual knowledge, ability to solve problems or judgment in meeting situations found at work.

A multiple-choice question is normally one of three types—

- It can begin with an incomplete statement followed by several possible endings. You are to find the one ending which *best* completes the statement, although some of the others may not be entirely wrong.
- It can also be a complete statement in the form of a question which is answered by choosing one of the statements listed.
- It can be in the form of a problem – again you select the best answer.

Here is an example of a multiple-choice question with a discussion which should give you some clues as to the method for choosing the right answer:

When an employee has a complaint about his assignment, the action which will *best* help him overcome his difficulty is to

A. discuss his difficulty with his coworkers
B. take the problem to the head of the organization
C. take the problem to the person who gave him the assignment
D. say nothing to anyone about his complaint

In answering this question, you should study each of the choices to find which is best. Consider choice "A" – Certainly an employee may discuss his complaint with fellow employees, but no change or improvement can result, and the complaint remains unresolved. Choice "B" is a poor choice since the head of the organization probably does not know what assignment you have been given, and taking your problem to him is known as "going over the head" of the supervisor. The supervisor, or person who made the assignment, is the person who can clarify it or correct any injustice. Choice "C" is, therefore, correct. To say nothing, as in choice "D," is unwise. Supervisors have and interest in knowing the problems employees are facing, and the employee is seeking a solution to his problem.

2) True/False Questions

The "true/false" or "right/wrong" form of question is sometimes used. Here a complete statement is given. Your job is to decide whether the statement is right or wrong.

SAMPLE: A roaming cell-phone call to a nearby city costs less than a non-roaming call to a distant city.

This statement is wrong, or false, since roaming calls are more expensive.

This is not a complete list of all possible question forms, although most of the others are variations of these common types. You will always get complete directions for answering questions. Be sure you understand *how* to mark your answers – ask questions until you do.

V. RECORDING YOUR ANSWERS

Computer terminals are used more and more today for many different kinds of exams.

For an examination with very few applicants, you may be told to record your answers in the test booklet itself. Separate answer sheets are much more common. If this separate answer sheet is to be scored by machine – and this is often the case – it is highly important that you mark your answers correctly in order to get credit.

An electronic scoring machine is often used in civil service offices because of the speed with which papers can be scored. Machine-scored answer sheets must be marked with a pencil, which will be given to you. This pencil has a high graphite content which responds to the electronic scoring machine. As a matter of fact, stray dots may register as answers, so do not let your pencil rest on the answer sheet while you are pondering the correct answer. Also, if your pencil lead breaks or is otherwise defective, ask for another.

Since the answer sheet will be dropped in a slot in the scoring machine, be careful not to bend the corners or get the paper crumpled.

The answer sheet normally has five vertical columns of numbers, with 30 numbers to a column. These numbers correspond to the question numbers in your test booklet. After each number, going across the page are four or five pairs of dotted lines. These short dotted lines have small letters or numbers above them. The first two pairs may also have a "T" or "F" above the letters. This indicates that the first two pairs only are to be used if the questions are of the true-false type. If the questions are multiple choice, disregard the "T" and "F" and pay attention only to the small letters or numbers.

Answer your questions in the manner of the sample that follows:

32. The largest city in the United States is
    - A. Washington, D.C.
    - B. New York City
    - C. Chicago
    - D. Detroit
    - E. San Francisco

1) Choose the answer you think is best. (New York City is the largest, so "B" is correct.)
2) Find the row of dotted lines numbered the same as the question you are answering. (Find row number 32)
3) Find the pair of dotted lines corresponding to the answer. (Find the pair of lines under the mark "B.")
4) Make a solid black mark between the dotted lines.

VI. BEFORE THE TEST

Common sense will help you find procedures to follow to get ready for an examination. Too many of us, however, overlook these sensible measures. Indeed, nervousness and fatigue have been found to be the most serious reasons why applicants fail to do their best on civil service tests. Here is a list of reminders:

- Begin your preparation early – Don't wait until the last minute to go scurrying around for books and materials or to find out what the position is all about.
- Prepare continuously – An hour a night for a week is better than an all-night cram session. This has been definitely established. What is more, a night a week for a month will return better dividends than crowding your study into a shorter period of time.
- Locate the place of the exam – You have been sent a notice telling you when and where to report for the examination. If the location is in a different town or otherwise unfamiliar to you, it would be well to inquire the best route and learn something about the building.
- Relax the night before the test – Allow your mind to rest. Do not study at all that night. Plan some mild recreation or diversion; then go to bed early and get a good night's sleep.
- Get up early enough to make a leisurely trip to the place for the test – This way unforeseen events, traffic snarls, unfamiliar buildings, etc. will not upset you.
- Dress comfortably – A written test is not a fashion show. You will be known by number and not by name, so wear something comfortable.
- Leave excess paraphernalia at home – Shopping bags and odd bundles will get in your way. You need bring only the items mentioned in the official notice you received; usually everything you need is provided. Do not bring reference books to the exam. They will only confuse those last minutes and be taken away from you when in the test room.
- Arrive somewhat ahead of time – If because of transportation schedules you must get there very early, bring a newspaper or magazine to take your mind off yourself while waiting.
- Locate the examination room – When you have found the proper room, you will be directed to the seat or part of the room where you will sit. Sometimes you are given a sheet of instructions to read while you are waiting. Do not fill out any forms until you are told to do so; just read them and be prepared.
- Relax and prepare to listen to the instructions
- If you have any physical problem that may keep you from doing your best, be sure to tell the test administrator. If you are sick or in poor health, you really cannot do your best on the exam. You can come back and take the test some other time.

VII. AT THE TEST

The day of the test is here and you have the test booklet in your hand. The temptation to get going is very strong. Caution! There is more to success than knowing the right answers. You must know how to identify your papers and understand variations in the type of short-answer question used in this particular examination. Follow these suggestions for maximum results from your efforts:

1) Cooperate with the monitor

The test administrator has a duty to create a situation in which you can be as much at ease as possible. He will give instructions, tell you when to begin, check to see that you are marking your answer sheet correctly, and so on. He is not there to guard you, although he will see that your competitors do not take unfair advantage. He wants to help you do your best.

2) Listen to all instructions

Don't jump the gun! Wait until you understand all directions. In most civil service tests you get more time than you need to answer the questions. So don't be in a hurry. Read each word of instructions until you clearly understand the meaning. Study the examples, listen to all announcements and follow directions. Ask questions if you do not understand what to do.

3) Identify your papers

Civil service exams are usually identified by number only. You will be assigned a number; you must not put your name on your test papers. Be sure to copy your number correctly. Since more than one exam may be given, copy your exact examination title.

4) Plan your time

Unless you are told that a test is a "speed" or "rate of work" test, speed itself is usually not important. Time enough to answer all the questions will be provided, but this does not mean that you have all day. An overall time limit has been set. Divide the total time (in minutes) by the number of questions to determine the approximate time you have for each question.

5) Do not linger over difficult questions

If you come across a difficult question, mark it with a paper clip (useful to have along) and come back to it when you have been through the booklet. One caution if you do this – be sure to skip a number on your answer sheet as well. Check often to be sure that you have not lost your place and that you are marking in the row numbered the same as the question you are answering.

6) Read the questions

Be sure you know what the question asks! Many capable people are unsuccessful because they failed to *read* the questions correctly.

7) Answer all questions

Unless you have been instructed that a penalty will be deducted for incorrect answers, it is better to guess than to omit a question.

8) Speed tests

It is often better NOT to guess on speed tests. It has been found that on timed tests people are tempted to spend the last few seconds before time is called in marking answers at random – without even reading them – in the hope of picking up a few extra points. To discourage this practice, the instructions may warn you that your score will be "corrected" for guessing. That is, a penalty will be applied. The incorrect answers will be deducted from the correct ones, or some other penalty formula will be used.

9) Review your answers

If you finish before time is called, go back to the questions you guessed or omitted to give them further thought. Review other answers if you have time.

10) Return your test materials

If you are ready to leave before others have finished or time is called, take ALL your materials to the monitor and leave quietly. Never take any test material with you. The monitor can discover whose papers are not complete, and taking a test booklet may be grounds for disqualification.

VIII. EXAMINATION TECHNIQUES

1) Read the general instructions carefully. These are usually printed on the first page of the exam booklet. As a rule, these instructions refer to the timing of the examination; the fact that you should not start work until the signal and must stop work at a signal, etc. If there are any *special* instructions, such as a choice of questions to be answered, make sure that you note this instruction carefully.

2) When you are ready to start work on the examination, that is as soon as the signal has been given, read the instructions to each question booklet, underline any key words or phrases, such as *least*, *best*, *outline*, *describe* and the like. In this way you will tend to answer as requested rather than discover on reviewing your paper that you *listed without describing*, that you selected the *worst* choice rather than the *best* choice, etc.

3) If the examination is of the objective or multiple-choice type – that is, each question will also give a series of possible answers: A, B, C or D, and you are called upon to select the best answer and write the letter next to that answer on your answer paper – it is advisable to start answering each question in turn. There may be anywhere from 50 to 100 such questions in the three or four hours allotted and you can see how much time would be taken if you read through all the questions before beginning to answer any. Furthermore, if you come across a question or group of questions which you know would be difficult to answer, it would undoubtedly affect your handling of all the other questions.

4) If the examination is of the essay type and contains but a few questions, it is a moot point as to whether you should read all the questions before starting to answer any one. Of course, if you are given a choice – say five out of seven and the like – then it is essential to read all the questions so you can eliminate the two that are most difficult. If, however, you are asked to answer all the questions, there may be danger in trying to answer the easiest one first because you may find that you will spend too much time on it. The best technique is to answer the first question, then proceed to the second, etc.

5) Time your answers. Before the exam begins, write down the time it started, then add the time allowed for the examination and write down the time it must be completed, then divide the time available somewhat as follows:

- If 3-1/2 hours are allowed, that would be 210 minutes. If you have 80 objective-type questions, that would be an average of 2-1/2 minutes per question. Allow yourself no more than 2 minutes per question, or a total of 160 minutes, which will permit about 50 minutes to review.
- If for the time allotment of 210 minutes there are 7 essay questions to answer, that would average about 30 minutes a question. Give yourself only 25 minutes per question so that you have about 35 minutes to review.

6) The most important instruction is to *read each question* and make sure you know what is wanted. The second most important instruction is to *time yourself properly* so that you answer every question. The third most important instruction is to *answer every question.* Guess if you have to but include something for each question. Remember that you will receive no credit for a blank and will probably receive some credit if you write something in answer to an essay question. If you guess a letter – say "B" for a multiple-choice question – you may have guessed right. If you leave a blank as an answer to a multiple-choice question, the examiners may respect your feelings but it will not add a point to your score. Some exams may penalize you for wrong answers, so in such cases *only*, you may not want to guess unless you have some basis for your answer.

7) Suggestions
   a. Objective-type questions
      1. Examine the question booklet for proper sequence of pages and questions
      2. Read all instructions carefully
      3. Skip any question which seems too difficult; return to it after all other questions have been answered
      4. Apportion your time properly; do not spend too much time on any single question or group of questions
      5. Note and underline key words – *all, most, fewest, least, best, worst, same, opposite,* etc.
      6. Pay particular attention to negatives
      7. Note unusual option, e.g., unduly long, short, complex, different or similar in content to the body of the question
      8. Observe the use of "hedging" words – *probably, may, most likely,* etc.
      9. Make sure that your answer is put next to the same number as the question
      10. Do not second-guess unless you have good reason to believe the second answer is definitely more correct
      11. Cross out original answer if you decide another answer is more accurate; do not erase until you are ready to hand your paper in
      12. Answer all questions; guess unless instructed otherwise
      13. Leave time for review

   b. Essay questions
      1. Read each question carefully
      2. Determine exactly what is wanted. Underline key words or phrases.
      3. Decide on outline or paragraph answer

4. Include many different points and elements unless asked to develop any one or two points or elements
5. Show impartiality by giving pros and cons unless directed to select one side only
6. Make and write down any assumptions you find necessary to answer the questions
7. Watch your English, grammar, punctuation and choice of words
8. Time your answers; don't crowd material

8) Answering the essay question

Most essay questions can be answered by framing the specific response around several key words or ideas. Here are a few such key words or ideas:

M's: manpower, materials, methods, money, management
P's: purpose, program, policy, plan, procedure, practice, problems, pitfalls, personnel, public relations

a. Six basic steps in handling problems:
   1. Preliminary plan and background development
   2. Collect information, data and facts
   3. Analyze and interpret information, data and facts
   4. Analyze and develop solutions as well as make recommendations
   5. Prepare report and sell recommendations
   6. Install recommendations and follow up effectiveness

b. Pitfalls to avoid
   1. *Taking things for granted* – A statement of the situation does not necessarily imply that each of the elements is necessarily true; for example, a complaint may be invalid and biased so that all that can be taken for granted is that a complaint has been registered
   2. *Considering only one side of a situation* – Wherever possible, indicate several alternatives and then point out the reasons you selected the best one
   3. *Failing to indicate follow up* – Whenever your answer indicates action on your part, make certain that you will take proper follow-up action to see how successful your recommendations, procedures or actions turn out to be
   4. *Taking too long in answering any single question* – Remember to time your answers properly

IX. AFTER THE TEST

Scoring procedures differ in detail among civil service jurisdictions although the general principles are the same. Whether the papers are hand-scored or graded by machine we have described, they are nearly always graded by number. That is, the person who marks the paper knows only the number – never the name – of the applicant. Not until all the papers have been graded will they be matched with names. If other tests, such as training and experience or oral interview ratings have been given, scores will be combined. Different parts of the examination usually have different weights. For example, the written test might count 60 percent of the final grade, and a rating of training and experience 40 percent. In many jurisdictions, veterans will have a certain number of points added to their grades.

After the final grade has been determined, the names are placed in grade order and an eligible list is established. There are various methods for resolving ties between those who get the same final grade – probably the most common is to place first the name of the person whose application was received first. Job offers are made from the eligible list in the order the names appear on it. You will be notified of your grade and your rank as soon as all these computations have been made. This will be done as rapidly as possible.

People who are found to meet the requirements in the announcement are called "eligibles." Their names are put on a list of eligible candidates. An eligible's chances of getting a job depend on how high he stands on this list and how fast agencies are filling jobs from the list.

When a job is to be filled from a list of eligibles, the agency asks for the names of people on the list of eligibles for that job. When the civil service commission receives this request, it sends to the agency the names of the three people highest on this list. Or, if the job to be filled has specialized requirements, the office sends the agency the names of the top three persons who meet these requirements from the general list.

The appointing officer makes a choice from among the three people whose names were sent to him. If the selected person accepts the appointment, the names of the others are put back on the list to be considered for future openings.

That is the rule in hiring from all kinds of eligible lists, whether they are for typist, carpenter, chemist, or something else. For every vacancy, the appointing officer has his choice of any one of the top three eligibles on the list. This explains why the person whose name is on top of the list sometimes does not get an appointment when some of the persons lower on the list do. If the appointing officer chooses the second or third eligible, the No. 1 eligible does not get a job at once, but stays on the list until he is appointed or the list is terminated.

X. HOW TO PASS THE INTERVIEW TEST

The examination for which you applied requires an oral interview test. You have already taken the written test and you are now being called for the interview test – the final part of the formal examination.

You may think that it is not possible to prepare for an interview test and that there are no procedures to follow during an interview. Our purpose is to point out some things you can do in advance that will help you and some good rules to follow and pitfalls to avoid while you are being interviewed.

What is an interview supposed to test?

The written examination is designed to test the technical knowledge and competence of the candidate; the oral is designed to evaluate intangible qualities, not readily measured otherwise, and to establish a list showing the relative fitness of each candidate – as measured against his competitors – for the position sought. Scoring is not on the basis of "right" and "wrong," but on a sliding scale of values ranging from "not passable" to "outstanding." As a matter of fact, it is possible to achieve a relatively low score without a single "incorrect" answer because of evident weakness in the qualities being measured.

Occasionally, an examination may consist entirely of an oral test – either an individual or a group oral. In such cases, information is sought concerning the technical knowledges and abilities of the candidate, since there has been no written examination for this purpose. More commonly, however, an oral test is used to supplement a written examination.

Who conducts interviews?

The composition of oral boards varies among different jurisdictions. In nearly all, a representative of the personnel department serves as chairman. One of the members of the board may be a representative of the department in which the candidate would work. In some cases, "outside experts" are used, and, frequently, a businessman or some other representative of the general public is asked to serve. Labor and management or other special groups may be represented. The aim is to secure the services of experts in the appropriate field.

However the board is composed, it is a good idea (and not at all improper or unethical) to ascertain in advance of the interview who the members are and what groups they represent. When you are introduced to them, you will have some idea of their backgrounds and interests, and at least you will not stutter and stammer over their names.

What should be done before the interview?

While knowledge about the board members is useful and takes some of the surprise element out of the interview, there is other preparation which is more substantive. It *is* possible to prepare for an oral interview – in several ways:

1) Keep a copy of your application and review it carefully before the interview

This may be the only document before the oral board, and the starting point of the interview. Know what education and experience you have listed there, and the sequence and dates of all of it. Sometimes the board will ask you to review the highlights of your experience for them; you should not have to hem and haw doing it.

2) Study the class specification and the examination announcement

Usually, the oral board has one or both of these to guide them. The qualities, characteristics or knowledges required by the position sought are stated in these documents. They offer valuable clues as to the nature of the oral interview. For example, if the job involves supervisory responsibilities, the announcement will usually indicate that knowledge of modern supervisory methods and the qualifications of the candidate as a supervisor will be tested. If so, you can expect such questions, frequently in the form of a hypothetical situation which you are expected to solve. NEVER go into an oral without knowledge of the duties and responsibilities of the job you seek.

3) Think through each qualification required

Try to visualize the kind of questions you would ask if you were a board member. How well could you answer them? Try especially to appraise your own knowledge and background in each area, *measured against the job sought*, and identify any areas in which you are weak. Be critical and realistic – do not flatter yourself.

4) Do some general reading in areas in which you feel you may be weak

For example, if the job involves supervision and your past experience has NOT, some general reading in supervisory methods and practices, particularly in the field of human relations, might be useful. Do NOT study agency procedures or detailed manuals. The oral board will be testing your understanding and capacity, not your memory.

5) Get a good night's sleep and watch your general health and mental attitude

You will want a clear head at the interview. Take care of a cold or any other minor ailment, and of course, no hangovers.

What should be done on the day of the interview?

Now comes the day of the interview itself. Give yourself plenty of time to get there. Plan to arrive somewhat ahead of the scheduled time, particularly if your appointment is in the fore part of the day. If a previous candidate fails to appear, the board might be ready for you a bit early. By early afternoon an oral board is almost invariably behind schedule if there are many candidates, and you may have to wait. Take along a book or magazine to read, or your application to review, but leave any extraneous material in the waiting room when you go in for your interview. In any event, relax and compose yourself.

The matter of dress is important. The board is forming impressions about you – from your experience, your manners, your attitude, and your appearance. Give your personal appearance careful attention. Dress your best, but not your flashiest. Choose conservative, appropriate clothing, and be sure it is immaculate. This is a business interview, and your appearance should indicate that you regard it as such. Besides, being well groomed and properly dressed will help boost your confidence.

Sooner or later, someone will call your name and escort you into the interview room. *This is it.* From here on you are on your own. It is too late for any more preparation. But remember, you asked for this opportunity to prove your fitness, and you are here because your request was granted.

What happens when you go in?

The usual sequence of events will be as follows: The clerk (who is often the board stenographer) will introduce you to the chairman of the oral board, who will introduce you to the other members of the board. Acknowledge the introductions before you sit down. Do not be surprised if you find a microphone facing you or a stenotypist sitting by. Oral interviews are usually recorded in the event of an appeal or other review.

Usually the chairman of the board will open the interview by reviewing the highlights of your education and work experience from your application – primarily for the benefit of the other members of the board, as well as to get the material into the record. Do not interrupt or comment unless there is an error or significant misinterpretation; if that is the case, do not hesitate. But do not quibble about insignificant matters. Also, he will usually ask you some question about your education, experience or your present job – partly to get you to start talking and to establish the interviewing "rapport." He may start the actual questioning, or turn it over to one of the other members. Frequently, each member undertakes the questioning on a particular area, one in which he is perhaps most competent, so you can expect each member to participate in the examination. Because time is limited, you may also expect some rather abrupt switches in the direction the questioning takes, so do not be upset by it. Normally, a board member will not pursue a single line of questioning unless he discovers a particular strength or weakness.

After each member has participated, the chairman will usually ask whether any member has any further questions, then will ask you if you have anything you wish to add. Unless you are expecting this question, it may floor you. Worse, it may start you off on an extended, extemporaneous speech. The board is not usually seeking more information. The question is principally to offer you a last opportunity to present further qualifications or to indicate that you have nothing to add. So, if you feel that a significant qualification or characteristic has been overlooked, it is proper to point it out in a sentence or so. Do not compliment the board on the thoroughness of their examination – they have been sketchy, and you know it. If you wish, merely say, "No thank you, I have nothing further to add." This is a point where you can "talk yourself out" of a good impression or fail to present an important bit of information. Remember, *you close the interview yourself.*

The chairman will then say, "That is all, Mr. ______, thank you." Do not be startled; the interview is over, and quicker than you think. Thank him, gather your belongings and take your leave. Save your sigh of relief for the other side of the door.

How to put your best foot forward

Throughout this entire process, you may feel that the board individually and collectively is trying to pierce your defenses, seek out your hidden weaknesses and embarrass and confuse you. Actually, this is not true. They are obliged to make an appraisal of your qualifications for the job you are seeking, and they want to see you in your best light. Remember, they must interview all candidates and a non-cooperative candidate may become a failure in spite of their best efforts to bring out his qualifications. Here are 15 suggestions that will help you:

1) Be natural – Keep your attitude confident, not cocky

If you are not confident that you can do the job, do not expect the board to be. Do not apologize for your weaknesses, try to bring out your strong points. The board is interested in a positive, not negative, presentation. Cockiness will antagonize any board member and make him wonder if you are covering up a weakness by a false show of strength.

2) Get comfortable, but don't lounge or sprawl

Sit erectly but not stiffly. A careless posture may lead the board to conclude that you are careless in other things, or at least that you are not impressed by the importance of the occasion. Either conclusion is natural, even if incorrect. Do not fuss with your clothing, a pencil or an ashtray. Your hands may occasionally be useful to emphasize a point; do not let them become a point of distraction.

3) Do not wisecrack or make small talk

This is a serious situation, and your attitude should show that you consider it as such. Further, the time of the board is limited – they do not want to waste it, and neither should you.

4) Do not exaggerate your experience or abilities

In the first place, from information in the application or other interviews and sources, the board may know more about you than you think. Secondly, you probably will not get away with it. An experienced board is rather adept at spotting such a situation, so do not take the chance.

5) If you know a board member, do not make a point of it, yet do not hide it

Certainly you are not fooling him, and probably not the other members of the board. Do not try to take advantage of your acquaintanceship – it will probably do you little good.

6) Do not dominate the interview

Let the board do that. They will give you the clues – do not assume that you have to do all the talking. Realize that the board has a number of questions to ask you, and do not try to take up all the interview time by showing off your extensive knowledge of the answer to the first one.

7) Be attentive

You only have 20 minutes or so, and you should keep your attention at its sharpest throughout. When a member is addressing a problem or question to you, give him your undivided attention. Address your reply principally to him, but do not exclude the other board members.

8) Do not interrupt

A board member may be stating a problem for you to analyze. He will ask you a question when the time comes. Let him state the problem, and wait for the question.

9) Make sure you understand the question

Do not try to answer until you are sure what the question is. If it is not clear, restate it in your own words or ask the board member to clarify it for you. However, do not haggle about minor elements.

10) Reply promptly but not hastily

A common entry on oral board rating sheets is "candidate responded readily," or "candidate hesitated in replies." Respond as promptly and quickly as you can, but do not jump to a hasty, ill-considered answer.

11) Do not be peremptory in your answers

A brief answer is proper – but do not fire your answer back. That is a losing game from your point of view. The board member can probably ask questions much faster than you can answer them.

12) Do not try to create the answer you think the board member wants

He is interested in what kind of mind you have and how it works – not in playing games. Furthermore, he can usually spot this practice and will actually grade you down on it.

13) Do not switch sides in your reply merely to agree with a board member

Frequently, a member will take a contrary position merely to draw you out and to see if you are willing and able to defend your point of view. Do not start a debate, yet do not surrender a good position. If a position is worth taking, it is worth defending.

14) Do not be afraid to admit an error in judgment if you are shown to be wrong

The board knows that you are forced to reply without any opportunity for careful consideration. Your answer may be demonstrably wrong. If so, admit it and get on with the interview.

15) Do not dwell at length on your present job

The opening question may relate to your present assignment. Answer the question but do not go into an extended discussion. You are being examined for a *new* job, not your present one. As a matter of fact, try to phrase ALL your answers in terms of the job for which you are being examined.

Basis of Rating

Probably you will forget most of these "do's" and "don'ts" when you walk into the oral interview room. Even remembering them all will not ensure you a passing grade. Perhaps you did not have the qualifications in the first place. But remembering them will help you to put your best foot forward, without treading on the toes of the board members.

Rumor and popular opinion to the contrary notwithstanding, an oral board wants you to make the best appearance possible. They know you are under pressure – but they also want to see how you respond to it as a guide to what your reaction would be under the pressures of the job you seek. They will be influenced by the degree of poise you display, the personal traits you show and the manner in which you respond.

ABOUT THIS BOOK

This book contains tests divided into Examination Sections. Go through each test, answering every question in the margin. At the end of each test look at the answer key and check your answers. On the ones you got wrong, look at the right answer choice and learn. Do not fill in the answers first. Do not memorize the questions and answers, but understand the answer and principles involved. On your test, the questions will likely be different from the samples. Questions are changed and new ones added. If you understand these past questions you should have success with any changes that arise. Tests may consist of several types of questions. We have additional books on each subject should more study be advisable or necessary for you. Finally, the more you study, the better prepared you will be. This book is intended to be the last thing you study before you walk into the examination room. Prior study of relevant texts is also recommended. NLC publishes some of these in our Fundamental Series. Knowledge and good sense are important factors in passing your exam. Good luck also helps. So now study this Passbook, absorb the material contained within and take that knowledge into the examination. Then do your best to pass that exam.

EXAMINATION SECTION

EXAMINATION SECTION
TEST 1

DIRECTIONS: Each question or incomplete statement is followed by several suggested answers or completions. Select the one that BEST answers the question or completes the statement. *PRINT THE LETTER OF THE CORRECT ANSWER IN THE SPACE AT THE RIGHT.*

1. The specification states: *The value of each change order shall be computed separately by cost of labor and materials, plus equipment allowance, plus overhead and profit.* The MOST probable value of overhead and profit is ______% of the cost of labor and materials plus equipment allowance. 1.____

   A. 5 B. 15 C. 34 D. 55

2. In the specifications is an item: *Equipment Allowance: Shall include rental of necessary equipment plus 9% of this rental.* According to the above specification, if a piece of equipment rents for $35 per day, Equipment Allowance for this equipment rented for 11 days is MOST NEARLY 2.____

   A. $484.00 B. $378.42 C. $385.00 D. $419.65

3. A supplier quotes a list price of $172.00 less 15 and 10 percent for twelve tools. The ACTUAL cost for these twelve tools is MOST NEARLY 3.____

   A. $146 B. $132 C. $129 D. $112

4. Which one of the following is the PRIMARY object in drawing up a set of specifications for materials to be purchased? 4.____

   A. Control of quality
   B. Outline of intended use
   C. Establishment of standard sizes
   D. Location and method of inspection

5. In order to avoid disputes over payments for extra work in a contract for construction, the BEST procedure to follow would be to 5.____

   A. have contractor submit work progress reports daily
   B. insert a special clause in the contract specifications
   C. have a representative on the job at all times to verify conditions
   D. allocate a certain percentage of the cost of the job to cover such expenses

6. You wish to order sponges in the most economical manner. Keeping in mind that large sponges can be cut up into many smaller sizes, the one of the following that has the LEAST cost per cubic inch of sponge is ______ sponges @ ______. 6.____

   A. 2" x 4" x 6"; $.24
   B. 4" x 8" x 12"; $1.44
   C. 4" x 6" x 36"; $4.80
   D. 6" x 8" x 32"; $9.60

7. The cost of a certain job is broken down as follows: 7.____

Materials	$375
Rental of equipment	120
Labor	315

The percentage of the total cost of the job that can be charged to materials is MOST NEARLY ______%.

A. 40 B. 42 C. 44 D. 46

8. Partial payments to outside contractors are USUALLY based on the 8.____

A. breakdown estimate submitted after the contract was signed
B. actual cost of labor and material plus overhead and profit
C. estimate of work completed which is generally submitted periodically
D. estimate of material delivered to the job

9. Building contracts usually require that estimates for changes made in the field be submitted for approval before the work can start. 9.____
The MAIN reason for this requirement is to

A. make sure that the contractor understands the change
B. discourage such changes
C. keep the contractor honest
D. enable the department to control its expenses

10. If the cost of a broom went up from $4.00 to $6.00, the percent INCREASE in the original cost is 10.____

A. 20 B. 25 C. 33 1/3 D. 50

11. The AVERAGE of the numbers 3, 5, 7, 8, 12 is 11.____

A. 5 B. 6 C. 7 D. 8

12. The cost of 100 bags of cotton cleaning cloths, 89 pounds per bag, at 7 cents per pound is 12.____

A. $549.35 B. $623.00 C. $700.00 D. $890.00

13. If 5 1/2 bags of sweeping compound cost $55,00, then 6 1/2 bags would cost 13.____

A. $60.00 B. $62.50 C. $65.00 D. $67.00

14. The cost of cleaning supplies in a project averaged $330.00 a month during the first 8 months of the year. 14.____
How much can be spent each month for the last four months if the total amount that can be spent for cleaning supplies for the year is $3,880?

A. $124 B. $220 C. $310 D. $330

15. The cost of rawl plugs is $2.75 per gross. The cost of 2,448 rawl plugs is 15.____

A. $46.75 B. $47.25 C. $47.75 D. $48.25

16. A caretaker received $70.00 for having worked from Monday through Friday, 9 A.M. to 5 P.M. with one hour a day for lunch. 16.____
The number of hours the caretaker would have to work to earn $12.00 is

A. 10
B. 6
C. 70 divided by 12
D. 70 minus 12

17. Assume that an employee is paid at the rate of $5.43 per hour with time and a half for overtime past 40 hours in a week. 17.____
If he works 43 hours in a week, his gross weekly pay is

A. $217.20 B. $219.20 C. $229.59 D. $241.64

18. Kerosene costs 36 cents a quart. 18.____
At that rate, two gallons would cost

A. $1.44 B. $2.16 C. $2.88 D. $3.60

Questions 19-21.

DIRECTIONS: Questions 19 through 21 are to be answered on the basis of the following table.

	Man Days Borough 1		Man Days Borough 2		Man Days Borough 3		Man Days Borough 4	
	Oct.	Nov.	Oct.	Nov.	Oct.	Nov.	Oct.	Nov.
Carpenter	70	100	35	180	145	205	120	85
Plumber	95	135	195	100	70	130	135	80
House Painter	90	90	120	80	85	85	95	195
Electrician	120	110	135	155	120	95	70	205
Blacksmith	125	145	60	180	205	145	80	125

19. In accordance with the above table, if the average daily pay of the five trades listed above is $47.50, the approximate labor cost of work done by the five trades during the month of October for Borough 1 is MOST NEARLY 19.____

A. $22,800 B. $23,450 C. $23,750 D. $26,125

20. In accordance with the above table, the Borough which MOST NEARLY made up 22.4% of the total plumbing work force for the month of November is Borough 20.____

A. 1 B. 2 C. 3 D. 4

21. In accordance with the above table, the average man days per month per Borough spent on electrical work for all Boroughs combined is MOST NEARLY 21.____

A. 120 B. 126 C. 130 D. 136

22. When preparing an estimate for a certain repair job, you determine that $125 worth of materials and 220 man-hours are required to complete the job. 22.____
If your man-hour cost is $5.25 per hour, the TOTAL cost of this repair job is

A. $1,030 B. $1,155 C. $1,280 D. $1,405

23. Assume that in determining the total cost of a repair job, a 15% shop cost is to be added to the costs of material and labor. 23.____
For a repair job which cost $200 in materials and $600 in labor, the shop cost is

A. $30 B. $60 C. $90 D. $120

24. Assume that in quantity purchases, the city receives a discount of 33 1/3%. 24.____
If a one gallon can of paint retails at $5.33 per gallon, the cost of 375 gallons of this paint is MOST NEARLY

A. $1,332.50 B. $1,332.75 C. $1,333.00 D. $1,333.25

25. Assume that eight barrels of cement together weigh a total of 3004 lbs. and 12 oz. 25.____
If there are four bags of cement per barrel, then the weight of one bag of cement is HOST NEARLY _______ lbs.

A. 93.1 B. 93.5 C. 93.9 D. 94.3

26. Lumber is usually sold by the board foot, and a board foot is defined as a board one foot square and one inch thick. 26.____
If the price of one board foot of lumber is 18 cents and you need 20 feet of lumber 6 inches wide and 1 inch thick, the cost of the 20 feet of lumber is

A. $1.80 B. $2.40 C. $3.60 D. $4.80

27. Assume that a trench is 42" wide, 5' deep, and 100' long. If the unit price of excavating the trench is $35 per cubic yard, the cost of excavating the trench is MOST NEARLY 27.____

A. $2,275 B. $5,110 C. $7,000 D. $21,000

28. No single activity has a very large effect on the final price of the complete housing structure and, therefore, the total cost is not affected appreciably by the price policy of any component. 28.____
From the above statement, you may conclude that

A. we cannot hope for substantial reductions in housing costs
B. the builder must assume responsibility for the high cost of construction
C. a 10% reduction in the cost of materials would result in much less than a 10% reduction in the cost of housing
D. federal government financing would reduce the city's cost of public housing

29. Four board feet of lumber, listed at $350 per M, will cost 29.____

A. $3.50 B. $1.40 C. $1.80 D. $4.00

30. The cost of material is approximately 3/8ths of the total cost of a certain job. 30.____
If the total cost of the job is $127.56, then the cost of material is MOST NEARLY

A. $47.83 B. $48.24 C. $48.65 D. $49.06

31. It takes four men six days to do a certain job. Working at the same speed, the number of days it will take three men to do this job is 31.____

A. 7 B. 8 C. 9 D. 10

32. A contractor on a large construction project USUALLY receives partial payments based on 32.____

A. estimates of completed work
B. actual cost of materials delivered and work completed
C. estimates of material delivered and not paid for by the contractor
D. the breakdown estimate submitted after the contract was signed and prorated over the estimated duration of the contract

33. In estimating the cost of a reinforced concrete structure, the contractor would be LEAST concerned with 33.____

A. volume of concrete
B. surface area of forms
C. pounds of reinforcing steel
D. type of coarse aggregate

34. Assume that an employee is paid at the rate of $6.25 per hour with time and a half for overtime past 40 hours in a week. 34.____
If she works 45 hours in a week, her gross weekly pay is

A. $285.49 B. $296.88 C. $301.44 D. $325.49

35. Cleaning fluid costs $1.19 a quart. 35.____
If there is a 10% discount for purchases over 5 gallons, how much will 8 gallons cost?

A. $34.28 B. $38.08 C. $42.28 D. $43.43

KEY (CORRECT ANSWERS)

1. B	11. C	26. A
2. D	12. B	27. A
3. B	13. C	28. C
4. A	14. C	29. B
5. C	15. A	30. A
6. B	16. B	31. B
7. D	17. D	32. A
8. C	18. C	33. D
9. D	19. C	34. B
10. D	20. B	35. A
	21. B	
	22. C	
	23. D	
	24. A	
	25. C	

TEST 2

DIRECTIONS: Each question or incomplete statement is followed by several suggested answers or completions. Select the one that BEST answers the question or completes the statement. *PRINT THE LETTER OF THE CORRECT ANSWER IN THE SPACE AT THE RIGHT.*

1. When windows are mounted side by side, the vertical piece between them is called the 1.____

   A. muntin B. casement C. sash D. mullion

2. Approximately how many pounds of 16d nails would be required for 1,000 square feet of floor framing area? 2.____

   A. 4-5 B. 7-8 C. 8-10 D. 10-12

3. What is represented by the electrical symbol shown at the right? 3.____

   A. Transformer
   B. Buzzer
   C. Telephone
   D. Bell

4. Which of the following structures would typically require a relatively higher grade of lumber? 4.____

   A. Vertical stud
   B. Joist
   C. Column
   D. Mud sill

5. A dump truck with a capacity of 10-12 cubic yards must load, drive, dump, and reposition itself over a 1-mile haul distance. 5.____
   What average amount of time should be estimated for this sequence?

   A. 15 minutes
   B. 30 minutes
   C. 1 hour
   D. 2 hours

6. The stripping of forms that are to be reused should be charged as 6.____

   A. common labor
   B. masonry labor
   C. carpentry labor
   D. material credit

7. What type of brick masonry unit is represented by the drawing shown at the right? 7.____

   A. Modular
   B. Norwegian
   C. 3 core
   D. Economy

2 2/3
4
8

8. Which of the following would be a typical thickness of a crushed-rock base course for an area of asphalt paving? 8.____

   A. 2" B. 5" C. 7" D. 10"

9. Which of the following wood floor materials would be MOST expensive to install? 9.____

A. Unfinished plank
B. Walnut parquet
C. Maple strip
D. Oak parquet

10. When calculating the air-conditioning needs for a building, a loss factor of _______ should be used for the exposure of walls to common heated surfaces. 10.____

A. 2.0
B. 3.5
C. 6.0
D. 7.5

11. Approximately how many linear feet of moldings, door and window trim, handrails, or similar parts can a carpenter install in a typical work day? 11.____

A. 100
B. 250
C. 400
D. 500

12. Which of the following constructions is NOT typically found in bathroom lavatories? 12.____

A. Enameled pressed steel
B. Cast iron
C. Cast ceramic
D. Stainless steel

13. What size reinforcing bar is typically used for masonry walls? 13.____

A. 3
B. 4
C. 7
D. 9

14. Which of the following would NOT be a typical source for a cost-per-square-foot estimate? 14.____

A. Architect
B. Engineer
C. Appraiser
D. Building contractor

15. Approximately how many stair treads with risers can a carpenter install in an average work day? 15.____

A. 5-8
B. 10-12
C. 15-18
D. 21-25

16. Each of the following materials is commonly used as sheet metal flashing for roof waterproofing EXCEPT 16.____

A. lead
B. galvanized steel
C. copper
D. zinc

17. The MOST commonly used type of metal lath for wall support is 17.____

A. self-furring
B. flat rib
C. flat diamond mesh
D. 3/8" rib

18. Approximately how long will it take to install a non-mortised lockset? 18.____

A. 15 minutes
B. 30 minutes
C. 1 hour
D. 2 hours

19. What is represented by the architectural symbol shown at the right? 19.____

A. Cut stone
B. Concrete block
C. Rubble stone
D. Brick

20. What type of nails are typically used for installing floor sheathing? 20.____

A. 4d
B. 8d
C. 12d
D. 16d

21. Each of the following is considered *finish* electrical work EXCEPT 21.____

A. outlet boxes
B. light fixtures
C. connection of fixtures to wiring
D. switches

22. Which component of cost estimating typically presents the GREATEST difficulty? 22.____

A. Materials
B. Overhead
C. Profit
D. Labor

23. Approximately how many hours will it take to install and caulk a typical sliding shower door assembly? 23.____

A. 2
B. 4
C. 6
D. 8

24. What is represented by the electrical symbol shown at the right? 24.____

A. Single pole switch
B. Lock or key switch
C. Service weather head
D. Main switch

25. Approximately how many exterior square feet can one painter cover, applying a primer coat and two coats of finish paint, in an average work day? 25.____

A. 100
B. 250
C. 350
D. 500

KEY (CORRECT ANSWERS)

1.	D	11.	B
2.	B	12.	D
3.	C	13.	B
4.	B	14.	C
5.	B	15.	C
6.	C	16.	A
7.	A	17.	C
8.	B	18.	B
9.	B	19.	A
10.	B	20.	B

21. A
22. D
23. B
24. A
25. D

TEST 3

DIRECTIONS: Each question or incomplete statement is followed by several suggested answers or completions. Select the one that BEST answers the question or completes the statement. *PRINT THE LETTER OF THE CORRECT ANSWER IN THE SPACE AT THE RIGHT.*

1. Irregular shapes and narrow lites typically reduce the rate of glass installation by ______%. 1.____

   A. 10-20 B. 25-35 C. 30-50 D. 55-75

2. What is represented by the electrical symbol shown at the right? 2.____

   A. Exposed wiring B. Fusible element
   C. Three-way switch D. Circuit breaker

3. Approximately how many square feet of siding can be installed by a crew in a typical work day? 3.____

   A. 250 B. 500 C. 750 D. 1,000

4. What is the construction term for hinges used on doors? 4.____

   A. Gables B. Butts C. Hips D. Plates

5. Floor joists are typically spaced about ______ apart. 5.____

   A. 16" B. 2 feet C. 3 feet D. 4 feet

6. Which of the following paving materials is generally MOST expensive? 6.____

   A. Brick on sand bed B. Random flagstone
   C. Asphalt D. Concrete

7. Approximately how long should it take a 2-person crew to install floor joists for a 100 square-foot area of floor space? 7.____

   A. 30 minutes B. 1 hour
   C. 3 hours D. 1 work day

8. A ______ is represented by the mechanical symbol shown at the right. 8.____

   A. pressure-reducing valve B. motor-operated valve
   C. lock and shield valve D. globe valve

9. On average, labor costs for a job will be about ______% of the total job cost. 9.____

   A. 15 B. 35 C. 55 D. 85

10. Most exterior paint averages a coverage of about ______ square feet per gallon. 10.____

   A. 100 B. 250 C. 400 D. 550

11. What type of window includes two sashes which slide vertically? 11.____

A. Double-hung
B. Screen
C. Casement
D. Sliding

12. Approximately how many linear feet of drywall tape can be applied during an average work day? 12.____

A. 250
B. 400
C. 750
D. 1,000

13. What is used to join lengths of copper pipe? 13.____

A. Molten solder
B. Threaded ends and sealer
C. Nipples
D. Lead-and-oakum seal

14. Typically, one gallon of prepared wallpaper paste will supply adhesive for ______ full rolls of wall covering. 14.____

A. 8
B. 12
C. 24
D. 36

15. What is represented by the electrical symbol shown at the right? 15.____

A. Range outlet
B. Wall bracket light fixture
C. Split-wired receptacle
D. Special purpose outlet

16. What size is MOST wire used in residential work? 16.____

A. 6
B. 8
C. 12
D. 16

17. Most fire codes require fire-resistant floor underneath fireplace units which extends to at least ______ inches beyond the unit. 17.____

A. 6
B. 12
C. 18
D. 24

18. If a building is constructed without a basement, ______ are typically used as footings. 18.____

A. joists
B. staked caissons
C. grade beams
D. mud sills

19. What is the MOST commonly used size range for flashing and gutter sheet metal? 19.____

A. 8-12
B. 14-18
C. 22-26
D. 24-30

20. Approximately how many square feet of interior wall space can one painter, using a brush, cover in an hour? 20.____

A. 25-50
B. 100
C. 175-200
D. 250

21. Which of the following downspout materials would be MOST expensive? 21.____

A. Copper
B. Aluminum
C. Zinc
D. Stainless steel

22. What is represented by the mechanical symbol shown at the right? ⊖ 22.____

A. Expansion valve
B. Floor drain
C. Shower
D. Scale trap

23. Approximately how much lead (pounds) is required per joint in one sewer line lead-and-oakum seal? 23.____

A. 1/4
B. 1/2
C. 1 1/2
D. 3

24. Which of the following caulking materials is MOST expensive? 24.____

A. Neoprene
B. Butyl
C. Polyurethane
D. Latex

25. The assembly inside a tank toilet that controls the water supply is the 25.____

A. P trap
B. bell-and-spigot
C. gating
D. ball cock

KEY (CORRECT ANSWERS)

1. C
2. B
3. A
4. B
5. A
6. D
7. C
8. D
9. A
10. C
11. A
12. A
13. A
14. B
15. C
16. C
17. B
18. C
19. C
20. B
21. A
22. A
23. A
24. B
25. C

EXAMINATION SECTION
TEST 1

DIRECTIONS: Each question or incomplete statement is followed by several suggested answers or completions. Select the one that BEST answers the question or completes the statement. *PRINT THE LETTER OF THE CORRECT ANSWER IN THE SPACE AT THE RIGHT.*

1. Which of the following types of estimates is considered BEST for estimating the total cost of a job? 1.____

   A. Unit cost estimate
   B. Lump-sum amount
   C. Cost-per-square-foot estimate
   D. Quantity survey

2. The scale of a typical set of architectural drawings uses ______ to represent 1 foot. 2.____

   A. 1/8" B. 1/4" C. 1/2" D. 1"

3. A *square* in construction terms is an area of roofing that is ______ square feet. 3.____

   A. 40 B. 75 C. 100 D. 120

4. A ______ is represented by the mechanical symbol 4.____

   A. liquid pump
   B. water closet, flush valve
   C. compressor
   D. duct volume damper

5. Typically, a mud sill is bolted to a concrete foundation at intervals of ______ inches. 5.____

   A. 12-18 B. 18-36 C. 36-48 D. 48-60

6. For how many hours should an *A label* fire door be able to withstand continuous fire exposure? 6.____

   A. 3/4 B. 1 C. 1 1/2 D. 3

7. The current-carrying capacity of an electric device is USUALLY expressed in terms of 7.____

   A. voltage B. amperage C. gauge D. resistance

8. Construction drawings show *quantities* via each of the following EXCEPT 8.____

   A. plans B. sections
   C. specifications D. details

9. What type of window consists of two or more sashes, one or more of which are moved horizontally? 9.____

   A. Transom B. Sliding
   C. Casement D. Double-hung

10. If boards are to be used for floor sheathing, the amount for cut-off ends and waste should be figured as _______% more than the floor space area to be sheathed. 10.____

A. 5 B. 10 C. 20 D. 30

11. Grade B sheet glass can be used for glazing up to _______ square feet of area. 11.____

A. 10 B. 16 C. 24 D. 30

12. What is generally considered to be the MAXIMUM roof pitch allowable for the use of roll roofing? 12.____
_______ in 12.

A. 2 B. 4 C. 6 D. 8

13. What is represented by the architectural symbol shown at the right? 13.____

A. Stone concrete
B. Cinder concrete
C. Gravel
D. Plaster

14. For estimating purposes, construction sound control methods are divided into each of the following major types EXCEPT 14.____

A. construction with spaced studs and/or layered wall board
B. absorbing material applied over wall or ceiling surfaces
C. suspended ceilings
D. sound-dampening floor covering

15. What is used to cover the ends of rafters in a cornice construction? 15.____

A. Fascia
B. Hips
C. Shears
D. Butt joints

16. Which of the following steps in a grading-quantity estimation would be performed FIRST? 16.____

A. Determine approximate finish grade
B. Calculate difference between cut and fill
C. Estimate elevation of grid corners from contours
D. Average the elevation of each grid square

17. What amount of masonry should a bricklayer and tender be able to install in an average work day? 17.____

A. 50 square feet
B. 100 square feet
C. 50 cubic feet
D. 100 linear feet

18. The time required for the placement labor and staking of slab-on-grade foundation forms should be calculated at APPROXIMATELY _______ hour(s) for 100 linear feet. 18.____

A. 1/2 B. 1 C. 2 1/2 D. 3 1/2

19. What is represented by the mechanical symbol shown at the right? 19.____

A. Wall air outlet
B. Clean out
C. Duct volume damper
D. Blower

20. What is the term for a steel pipe filled with concrete and used as a beam support? 20.____

A. Bearing column
B. Platform frame
C. Lally column
D. Soffit

21. Which of the following types of wood windows would be MOST expensive to install? 21.____

A. Awning
B. Casement
C. Double-hung
D. Horizontal sliding

22. A workman is installing 3 1/2-inch-thick batts of R-11 fiberglass insulation. About how many square feet will the workman be able to install in a typical work day? 22.____

A. 300-500 B. 650-1000 C. 1200-1500 D. 1750-2000

23. What is represented by the architectural symbol shown at the right? 23.____

A. Cast iron
B. Aluminum
C. Steel
D. Brick

24. Most rafters are spaced _______ inches apart. 24.____

A. 18 B. 24 C. 36 D. 48

25. What is the dividing strip within a window assembly that separates the various panes of glass? 25.____

A. Muntin B. Sash C. Bunting D. Mullion

KEY (CORRECT ANSWERS)

1.	D	11.	B
2.	B	12.	B
3.	C	13.	B
4.	A	14.	D
5.	D	15.	A
6.	D	16.	C
7.	B	17.	B
8.	C	18.	D
9.	B	19.	C
10.	C	20.	C

21. C
22. C
23. C
24. B
25. A

TEST 2

DIRECTIONS: Each question or incomplete statement is followed by several suggested answers or completions. Select the one that BEST answers the question or completes the statement. *PRINT THE LETTER OF THE CORRECT ANSWER IN THE SPACE AT THE RIGHT.*

1. What type of brick masonry unit is represented by the drawing shown at the right? 1.____
   A. Norman
   B. Economy
   C. King Norman
   D. Double

4
12
4

2. The typical thickness of asphalt paving, applied over a gravel base course, is 2.____

   A. 1/2-2" B. 1-3" C. 2-5" D. 3-7"

3. Which of the following waterproofing materials is LEAST expensive? 3.____

   A. Two-ply polyethylene (.002")
   B. Sprayed-on bituminous coating
   C. Two-ply felt membrane
   D. Elastomeric waterproofing (1/32")

4. Each of the following structures must always be included in an estimate if a *hip* roof is shown on drawings EXCEPT 4.____

   A. box cornice
   B. collar beam
   C. fascia
   D. solid sheathing

5. What is represented by the electrical symbol shown at the right? 5.____

   A. Special purpose outlet
   B. Transformer
   C. Paging system
   D. Telephone

6. The edge of a roof at the end of a building is called a 6.____

   A. sill B. cornice C. frieze D. rake

7. According to established finish-designation standards, which of the following finish materials would be ranked at the HIGHEST grade? 7.____

   A. White bronze
   B. Bright bronze
   C. Nickel-plated
   D. Cadmium-plated

8. What is represented by the electrical symbol shown at the right? 8.____

   A. Duplex receptacle
   B. Call system
   C. Wall bracket light fixture
   D. Ceiling light fixture

9. How many board-feet of rafters should two carpenters be able to install in a typical work day? 9.____

A. 250 B. 500 C. 800 D. 1200

10. The valve at the LOWEST point of a water system is the 10.____

A. drain cock
B. globe valve
C. check valve
D. ball cock

11. When purchasing siding, what percentage of the material should typically be calculated as waste? 11.____

A. 10% B. 15% C. 25% D. 35%

12. Which of the following is considered a *variable* overhead cost? 12.____

A. Business permit
B. Storage space
C. Job permit
D. Office utilities

13. What is the MOST commonly used paint base for use in kitchens and baths? 13.____

A. Oil latex
B. Oleoresin
C. Urethane
D. Alkyd enamel

14. Approximately how many linear feet of caulking material would be required for each door/ window opening? 14.____

A. 5-10 B. 12-15 C. 18-20 D. 22-28

15. What type of window is hinged at the side and opens outward from the opposite edge? 15.____

A. Awning B. Casement C. Storm D. Sliding

16. Approximately how many square feet of particle board floor underlayment can be installed by a crew in a normal work day? 16.____

A. 250 B. 750 C. 1200 D. 1500

17. What is represented by the architectural symbol shown at the right? 17.____

A. Earth B. Sand C. Plaster D. Fire brick

18. Approximately how many linear feet of drywall tape will be required for 1000 square feet of area? 18.____

A. 250 B. 400 C. 750 D. 1000

19. Which type of paving material can typically be applied MOST quickly? 19.____

A. Asphalt
B. Concrete, no curbs
C. Random flagstone
D. Concrete sidewalk

20. Approximately how many square feet of door and window surfaces should a painter be able to cover in one hour? 20.____

A. 50 B. 75 C. 125 D. 175

21. What is the term for the thin coat of plaster applied to masonry or concrete walls to obtain a watertight or smooth surface? 21.____

A. Plate B. Laminate C. Parging D. Cripple

22. For estimating the labor cost of the installation of countertops and sink splashes, the typical tile labor time should be multiplied by 22.____

A. 1/2 B. 2 C. 3 D. 4

23. In most retail stores, the markup for overhead profit is ______% over the wholesale cost of the material. 23.____

A. 7-10 B. 12-25 C. 33-50 D. 40-60

24. When making wall covering estimates, the general practice is to add ______% to the cost of materials to account for waste and pattern matching. 24.____

A. 10 B. 20 C. 35 D. 45

25. The underside of a cornice, beam, or any other material is known as a 25.____

A. screed B. section C. truss D. soffit

KEY (CORRECT ANSWERS)

1.	C	11.	A
2.	B	12.	C
3.	A	13.	D
4.	B	14.	C
5.	B	15.	B
6.	D	16.	D
7.	A	17.	A
8.	D	18.	B
9.	C	19.	A
10.	A	20.	C

21. C
22. C
23. C
24. B
25. D

TEST 3

DIRECTIONS: Each question or incomplete statement is followed by several suggested answers or completions. Select the one that BEST answers the question or completes the statement. *PRINT THE LETTER OF THE CORRECT ANSWER IN THE SPACE AT THE RIGHT.*

1. Approximately how many square feet of 4 1/4" x 4 1/4" glazed wall tile, applied with the adhesive-set method, can be applied in an average work day? 1.____

   A. 60 B. 130 C. 175 D. 220

2. Which of the following would NOT be a typical R-value for fiberglass roll insulation material? 2.____

   A. R-8 B. R-11 C. R-23 D. R-30

3. What is represented by the electrical symbol shown at the right? 3.____

   A. Signal push button
   B. Fluorescent light fixture
   C. Radio outlet
   D. Street light and bracket

4. Generally, finishing hardware costs will be a MAXIMUM of _______% of the total job cost. 4.____

   A. .5 B. 1 C. 3 D. 7

5. Built-up roofs are MOST often made from 5.____

   A. saturated felt
   B. tarpaper shingles
   C. wood shake
   D. tile

6. What is represented by the architectural symbol shown at the right? 6.____

   A. Cut stone
   B. Concrete blocK
   C. Rubble stone
   D. Brick

7. Most tubs, toilets, sinks, and lavatories require an average of ______ hours labor for the installation of rough plumbing. 7.____

   A. 3 B. 5 C. 7 D. 9

8. What is the term for the inclined members of a stair that support the other members? 8.____

   A. Stringers B. Slopes C. Slumps D. Risers

9. Approximately how many square yards of diamond metal lath wall support can be installed in a typical work day? 9.____

   A. 30-40 B. 50-60 C. 75-85 D. 85-100

10. What type of concrete masonry unit is represented by the drawing shown at the right? 10.____

    A. Double corner
    B. Soffit floor
    C. Corner
    D. Half cut header

11. Which of the following diameters would be MOST typical for a caisson hole? 11.____

A. 12-24" B. 30-36" C. 40-48" D. 60-72"

12. One bundle of six gypsum lath will cover an area of ______ square feet of wall space. 12.____

A. 18 B. 32 C. 48 D. 64

13. The estimate for cost of forms typically relies on 13.____

A. surface contact feet
B. cubic feet of foundation material
C. material used as studs
D. linear feet of forms

14. What is represented by the architectural symbol shown at the right? 14.____

A. Batted insulation
B. Vertical siding
C. Concrete block
D. Ceramic tile

15. Approximately how many square feet of finish plywood siding can be installed by two carpenters in a typical work day? 15.____

A. 200 B. 650 C. 850 D. 1200

16. After construction has begun, various fabricated items may require drawings that will indicate the exact size, shape, and material that the fabrication will have. These drawings are called 16.____

A. detail drawings
B. shop drawings
C. diagrams
D. specifications

17. How many bundles of roofing shakes, installed at 10" exposure, would be required to cover one square of roof area? 17.____

A. 1 B. 3 C. 5 D. 7

18. What type of labor will normally be calculated for waterproofing work? 18.____

A. Carpentry
B. Roofing
C. Common labor
D. Tile

19. Which of the following is NOT generally classified as *rough* plumbing? 19.____

A. Hot water line
B. Tub fixture
C. Vent stack
D. Gas piping

20. Approximately how many square feet of 20-year bonded flat roofing can be installed by a crew in an average work day? 20.____

A. 400-600
B. 750-1000
C. 1200-1600
D. 1800-2000

21. Approximately how many hours of labor will be required for the machine sanding of 1000 square feet of unfinished wood strip flooring? 21.____

A. 1/2 B. 1 C. 3 D. 4 1/2

22. What is represented by the mechanical symbol —▷◁— shown at the right? 22.____

A. Diaphragm valve
B. Lock and shield valve
C. Gate valve
D. Check valve

23. Approximately how many linear feet of mud sill should a 2-person crew be able to install in a typical work day? 23.____

A. 50-100 B. 150-250 C. 250-300 D. 350-400

24. When calculating the area of a gabled roof, the estimator should remember to multiply the initial figure by 24.____

A. 1/4 B. 1/2 C. 2 D. 4

25. The calculation of the square-foot area of a building includes the area of the 25.____

A. internal face
B. basement
C. attic
D. external face

KEY (CORRECT ANSWERS)

1. C
2. A
3. B
4. C
5. A

6. B
7. B
8. A
9. B
10. C

11. B
12. B
13. A
14. A
15. B

16. B
17. C
18. B
19. B
20. D

21. B
22. C
23. C
24. C
25. D

EXAMINATION SECTION
TEST 1

DIRECTIONS: Each question or incomplete statement is followed by several suggested answers or completions. Select the one that BEST answers the question or completes the statement. *PRINT THE LETTER OF THE CORRECT ANSWER IN THE SPACE AT THE RIGHT.*

1. A ______ would MOST likely be used to estimate the cost of additional yards of concrete, or additional lengths of piling. 1.____

   A. quantity survey
   B. lump-sum amount
   C. cost-per-square-foot estimate
   D. unit cost estimate

2. How many studs are usually required for 10 linear feet of wall, excluding openings and plates? 2.____

   A. 1   B. 5   C. 10   D. 12

3. What is represented by the mechanical symbol ☒ shown at the right? 3.____

   A. Supply duct   B. Gauge
   C. Exhaust duct   D. Floor drain

4. The excavation of compacted sand or gravel will require an angle of repose (slope) of 1 ft. vertical to ______ ft. horizontal. 4.____

   A. 3/4   B. 1   C. 1 1/2   D. 2

5. Which of the following types of tile for resilient flooring would be LEAST expensive? 5.____

   A. Pure vinyl   B. Asphalt
   C. Cork   D. Rubberized marbleized

6. What is the typical estimate (in linear feet) for two laborers' output per day of regular chain-link fencing? 6.____

   A. 50   B. 100   C. 150   D. 200

7. What is used between the ridge and valley rafters of a roof construction? 7.____

   A. Fascia   B. Hip rafter
   C. Packing   D. Jack rafter

8. Approximately how many square feet of surface area can be covered by 1 gallon of adhesive for resilient flooring sheet material? 8.____

   A. 75   B. 125   C. 200   D. 250

9. Water piping is NOT typically made of 9.____

   A. copper   B. cast iron
   C. galvanized steel   D. plastic

10. What is represented by the electrical symbol shown at the right? 10.____

A. Buzzer
B. Clock receptacle
C. Electric motor
D. Circuit breaker

11. Approximately how many linear feet of 1/4" copper pipe can be installed in a typical work day? 11.____

A. 35-40 B. 50-60 C. 65-75 D. 85-100

12. What is the term for short studs required beneath window framing, and at similar locations? 12.____

A. Scrap B. Cripple C. Hash D. Hips

13. For MOST brick work, scaffolding is required at intervals of about _______ feet. 13.____

A. 4 B. 6 C. 8 D. 10

14. What type of concrete masonry unit is represented by the drawing shown at the right? 14.____

A. Header
B. Stretcher
C. Channel
D. Bull nose

15. The movable portion of a window that contains the glass is the 15.____

A. cornice B. sash C. scale D. pane

16. Approximately how many hours of labor will be required for the installation of 100 square feet of countertop ceramic tile and a 6" back splash? 16.____

A. 3 B. 5 C. 8 D. 12

17. Which of the following types of wall constructions will be LEAST able to dampen the transmission of sound? 17.____

A. Single-stud gypsum board
B. Metal-stud plaster on lath
C. Single-stud plaster on gypsum board
D. Staggered-stud gypsum board

18. What is represented by the mechanical symbol shown at the right? 18.____

A. Return duct
B. Shower
C. Corner tub
D. Water or fuel tank

19. Which of the following types of aluminum windows would be MOST expensive to install? 19.____

A. Horizontal sliding
B. Casement
C. Double-hung
D. Projected vent

20. Generally, an adequate interest or profit return from a construction job must be more than ______ %. 20.____

A. 3-5 B. 7-10 C. 12-22 D. 24-45

21. Which of the following types of doors would be LEAST expensive? 21.____

A. Hollow core, birch-veneer face
B. Solid-core, walnut-faced
C. Hollow core, hardboard-faced
D. Solid-core, birch-veneer face

22. What is represented by the architectural symbol shown at the right? 22.____

A. Shingle roofing
B. Aluminum
C. Structural metal
D. Cast iron

23. Approximately how many hours should be estimated for the trimming of a door blank (3'x7' wood door), plus the installation of frame and trim? 23.____

A. 1 B. 2 C. 4 D. 6

24. Which of the following types of wire enclosures is NOT currently in use? 24.____

A. Romex
B. Conduit
C. Flexible cable
D. Knob-in-tube

25. If precut granite block is used for curbs, the cost will be roughly ______ % more than the cost for using concrete. 25.____

A. 10 B. 30 C. 50 D. 70

KEY (CORRECT ANSWERS)

1. D
2. C
3. A
4. C
5. B

6. C
7. D
8. C
9. B
10. C

11. B
12. B
13. A
14. B
15. B

16. D
17. A
18. D
19. B
20. B

21. C
22. D
23. C
24. D
25. C

TEST 2

DIRECTIONS: Each question or incomplete statement is followed by several suggested answers or completions. Select the one that BEST answers the question or completes the statement. *PRINT THE LETTER OF THE CORRECT ANSWER IN THE SPACE AT THE RIGHT.*

1. In an average work day, approximately how many cubic yards of earth can be excavated by means of a tractor shovel with a 1-yard bucket? 1.____

   A. 10 B. 75 C. 350 D. 500

2. Mesh reinforcing material is MOST commonly used in 2.____

   A. vertical walls
   B. supports
   C. slabs
   D. footings

3. What is represented by the architectural symbol shown at the right? 3.____

   A. Cut stone
   B. Concrete block
   C. Rubble stone
   D. Fire brick

4. Which of the following does NOT require an external trap that connects the sewer line? 4.____

   A. Kitchen sink
   B. Toilet
   C. Lavatory
   D. Tub

5. In one hour, a typical caisson boring machine will be able to bore ______ linear feet. 5.____

   A. 75 B. 125 C. 200 D. 250

6. Most bath accessories require about ______ to install. 6.____

   A. 15 minutes
   B. 45 minutes
   C. 1 hour
   D. 14 hours

7. What is represented by the electrical symbol shown at the right? 7.____

   A. Electric motor
   B. Bell
   C. Paging system
   D. Street light and bracket

8. Which of the following plumbing (pipe) materials would be MOST expensive to install? 8.____

   A. 3" galvanized steel
   B. 1/4" galvanized steel
   C. 1/4" copper tubing
   D. High-strength PVC plastic

9. The horizontal band of material directly beneath a cornice, and above the siding, is known as the 9.____

   A. gable B. section C. perimeter D. frieze

10. Approximately how many hours are typically required for carpenter labor to install 1,000 square feet of plywood floor sheathing? 10.____

    A. 1-3 B. 3-4 C. 5-6 D. 7-8

11. The generally accepted method for figuring *in-place* costs for small accessories such as doorbells, smoke alarms, and garage door openers is to multiply the material cost by 11.____

A. 4 B. 2 C. 3 D. 4

12.____

12. A ______ is represented by the mechanical symbol shown at the right.

A. diaphragm valve
B. lock and shield valve
C. gate valve
D. check valve

13. What is used to join lengths of galvanized steel pipe? 13.____

A. Molten solder
B. Threaded ends and sealer
C. Elbows
D. Lead-and-oakum seal

14. Approximately how much plumber's labor would be required for the installation of a single chrome-plated faucet set? 14.____

A. 15 minutes
B. 30 minutes
C. 1 hour
D. 1 1/2 hours

15. Each of the following roof flashing materials takes about the same amount of time to install EXCEPT 15.____

A. aluminum
B. galvanized steel
C. zinc alloy
D. stainless steel

16. What is the MOST commonly used grade of asphalt tile used for resilient flooring? 16.____

A. A B. B C. C D. D

17. Which of the following plastic pipe materials is usable for hot water lines? 17.____

A. DWV B. ABS C. PVC D. PVDC

18. Approximately how many linear feet of gutter material can be installed by one person in an average work day? 18.____

A. 80 B. 120 C. 150 D. 175

19.____

19. What is represented by the electrical symbol shown at the right?

A. Junction box
B. Blanked outlet
C. Television outlet
D. Buzzer

20. When estimating the cost of resilient flooring material, how much floor tile and base should be calculated as waste? 20.____

A. 5% B. 10% C. 20% D. 30%

21. Most fire codes suggest that wall surfaces within ______ of a fireplace unit be covered with a fire-retardant surface. 21.____

A. 8 inches B. 16 inches C. 4 feet D. 8 feet

22. Wood, gypsum board, or expanded metal used as a base for plaster finish is known as 22.____

A. parging B. lath C. chord D. aggregate

23. Approximately how many linear feet of sewer pipe can be installed in an average work day? 23.____

A. 25 B. 50 C. 75 D. 100

24. Approximately how many square feet of board floor sheathing can be installed by a crew in a normal work day? 24.____

A. 250 B. 500 C. 750 D. 1,000

25. A ______ line is represented by the mechanical ______ symbol shown at the right. 25.____

A. soil
B. refrigerant
C. cold water
D. hot water

KEY (CORRECT ANSWERS)

1. C
2. C
3. C
4. B
5. B

6. A
7. B
8. A
9. D
10. D

11. B
12. A
13. B
14. C
15. A

16. C
17. D
18. B
19. D
20. B

21. A
22. B
23. B
24. C
25. D

TEST 3

DIRECTIONS: Each question or incomplete statement is followed by several suggested answers or completions. Select the one that BEST answers the question or completes the statement. *PRINT THE LETTER OF THE CORRECT ANSWER IN THE SPACE AT THE RIGHT.*

1. Which of the following plumbing (pipe) materials would be LEAST expensive to install? 1.____

   A. 1/4" galvanized steel
   B. 1" copper pipe
   C. 1/4" copper tubing
   D. High-strength PVC plastic

2. Which of the following roof flashing materials would take the GREATEST amount of time to install? 2.____

   A. Aluminum
   B. Stainless steel
   C. Zinc alloy
   D. Copper

3. Approximately how many square feet of *Venetian* blind window accessory can be installed by a worker in an average day? 3.____

   A. 50 B. 100 C. 225 D. 450

4. What is the term for a short length of pipe threaded at each end and used to connect fittings? 4.____

   A. Joist B. Nipple C. ABS D. Elbow

5. Approximately how many square yards of metal lathing work can be installed for a ceiling in a typical work day? 5.____

   A. 30-40 B. 50-60 C. 60-80 D. 85-100

6. The approximate weight specification for a 20-year bonded flat roof is _______ pounds per square foot of roof area. 6.____

   A. 3 B. 6 C. 9 D. 12

7. Approximately how many linear feet of PVC pipe can be installed in a typical work day? 7.____

   A. 35-40 B. 50-60 C. 65-75 D. 85-100

8. Each of the following is a primary factor in the pricing of finishing hardware EXCEPT 8.____

   A. finish B. size C. quality D. use

9. What is the nominal length, in inches, of most ordered studs? 9.____

   A. 48 B. 60 C. 72 D. 96

10. The bottom member of a window assembly, which forms the sill, is the 10.____

    A. stringer B. riser C. slump D. stool

11. For how many hours should a *D label* fire door be able to withstand continuous fire exposure? 11.____

    A. 3/4 B. 1 C. 1 1/2 D. 3

12. What type of window frame is anodized? 12.____

A. Steel B. Aluminum C. Bronze D. Wood

13. On average, the cost of materials for a job will be about ______ % of the total job cost. 13.____

A. 15 B. 35 C. 55 D. 85

14. Each of the following means is used to secure vertical metal studs to wall plates EXCEPT 14.____

A. sheet metal screws
B. spot welding
C. tie wire
D. soldering

15. How much time should be estimated for the installation of a fire door and frame? 15.____

A. 30 minutes
B. 1 hour
C. 2 hours
D. 4 hours

16. Which of the following would NOT be a color of grade A asphalt tile? 16.____

A. Black B. Green C. Yellow D. Brown

17. Concrete for on-grade floor installations should typically have an aggregate size of not more than ______ inch. 17.____

A. 1/4 B. 1/2 C. 3/4 D. 1

18. Which type of estimate is MOST often used with change orders? 18.____

A. Quantity survey
B. Lump-sum amount
C. Cost-per-square-foot estimate
D. Unit cost estimate

19. Which of the following types of glass will be LEAST expensive? 19.____

A. Grade B sheet
B. 1/4" wire glass
C. Mirror
D. 1/8" patterned *obscure* glass

20. According to established finish-designation standards, which of the following finish materials would be ranked at the HIGHEST grade? 20.____

A. Chromium-plated
B. Bright bronze
C. Stainless steel
D. Lacquered satin aluminum

21.____

21. What is represented by the mechanical symbol shown at the right?

A. Door
B. Scale trap
C. Strainer
D. T connection

22. Most metal roofs require a waterproof underlayment that weighs about _______ pounds per 100 square feet of roof area. 22.____

A. 30 B. 60 C. 100 D. 125

23. A material used over a rough subfloor that will provide a smooth surface for the finish floor is termed a(n) 23.____

A. soffit
B. underlayment
C. vapor barrier
D. molding

24. Approximately how many square feet of wood strip flooring can be installed in one hour? 24.____

A. 50 B. 125 C. 225 D. 300

25. The scale of a typical site plans uses 1/4" to represent 25.____

A. 1 inch B. 1 foot C. 25 feet D. 100 feet

KEY (CORRECT ANSWERS)

1. C
2. D
3. D
4. B
5. C

6. B
7. A
8. B
9. D
10. D

11. C
12. B
13. D
14. D
15. B

16. C
17. C
18. B
19. A
20. C

21. C
22. A
23. B
24. D
25. D

EXAMINATION SECTION
TEST 1

DIRECTIONS: Each question or incomplete statement is followed by several suggested answers or completions. Select the one that BEST answers the question or completes the statement. *PRINT THE LETTER OF THE CORRECT ANSWER IN THE SPACE AT THE RIGHT.*

1. What is represented by the architectural symbol shown at the right? 1.____

   A. Stone concrete
   B. Cinder concrete
   C. Gravel
   D. Plaster

2. Poured installation of fiberglass or mineral wool insulation material will typically occur at a rate of _______ cubic feet per day. 2.____

   A. 20 B. 80 C. 120 D. 180

3. What is the MOST effective method for backfilling excavated material? 3.____

   A. Sheepfoot roller
   B. Bulldozer
   C. Shoveling
   D. Pneumatic tamper

4. Approximately how many square feet of unfinished plank flooring can be installed in an average work day? 4.____

   A. 50 B. 150 C. 225 D. 300

5. Studs for concrete basement forms are typically spaced _______ apart. 5.____

   A. 18 inches B. 2 feet C. 4 feet D. 8 feet

6. Most construction stone is calculated and purchased by the 6.____

   A. square foot
   B. linear foot
   C. cubic yard
   D. ton

7. When earth backfill is replaced at a site, it is required to be compacted to within _______% of the original density. 7.____

   A. 65-75 B. 75-90 C. 85-95 D. 80-100

8. What type of brick masonry unit is represented by the drawing shown at the right? 8.____

   A. Norman
   B. Norwegian
   C. Corner
   D. Skippy

9. A laborer on a plain gable roof will typically install approximately _______ bundles of straight shingles in an average work day. 9.____

   A. 3-5 B. 6-9 C. 10-15 D. 17-20

10. What material is applied behind wall support mesh to reduce plaster waste? 10.____

A. Mastic
B. Gypsum board
C. Chicken wire
D. Asphalt-saturated felt

11. A ______ line is represented by the mechanical ______ symbol shown at the right. 11.____

A. fuel oil
B. vent
C. cold water
D. hot water

12. Approximately how many square feet of exterior surface can be prepared for paint or stain in one hour? 12.____

A. 50
B. 100
C. 150
D. 250

13. What tool is used to rough level concrete when it is still plastic? 13.____

A. Drum
B. Header
C. Float
D. Screed

14. Most stains that are applied to heavy timber can cover about ______ square feet per gallon. 14.____

A. 100
B. 250
C. 350
D. 550

15. Which of the following is NOT one of the three standard methods for installing glazed tile? 15.____

A. Furan resin grout
B. Full mortar beds
C. Organic adhesives
D. Dry-set thin cement

16. Generally, the cost for a buildings's heating/air conditioning make up about ______% of the total construction cost. 16.____

A. 1-3
B. 4-8
C. 5-10
D. 8-12

17. What is represented by the electrical symbol shown at the right? 17.____

S

A. Lock or key switch
B. Two-way switch
C. Switch with duplex receptacle
D. Triplex receptacle

18. Most structural lumber is considered *yard dry* at a MAXIMUM of about ______% moisture content. 18.____

A. 5
B. 10
C. 20
D. 30

19. What is the term for a wood or metal edge applied to the wall and used as a guide to determine the depth of plaster? 19.____

A. Rake
B. Float
C. Screed
D. Stud

20. Approximately how many single rolls of wall covering can be hung by one worker in a typical work day? 20.____

A. 12
B. 20
C. 30
D. 45

21. What is represented by the architectural symbol shown at the right? 21.____

A. Structural tile
B. Concrete block
C. Fire brick
D. Brick

22. Approximately how many square feet of interior wall space can one painter, using a roller, cover in an hour? 22.____

A. 25-50 B. 100 C. 175-200 D. 250

23. Cement plaster scratch coat for tile installation can typically be applied at a rate of ______ square yards per work day. 23.____

A. 150 B. 300 C. 500 D. 750

24. MOST gas lines are made of 24.____

A. black iron
B. copper
C. galvanized steel
D. plastic

25. For most types of resilient flooring installation, approximately how many hours of labor will be required to install 100 square feet? 25.____

A. 1/2 B. 1 C. 3 D. 4 1/2

KEY (CORRECT ANSWERS)

1. C
2. A
3. B
4. B
5. C

6. D
7. C
8. A
9. C
10. D

11. C
12. B
13. C
14. B
15. A

16. B
17. C
18. C
19. C
20. C

21. C
22. C
23. B
24. A
25. C

TEST 2

DIRECTIONS: Each question or incomplete statement is followed by several suggested answers or completions. Select the one that BEST answers the question or completes the Statement. *PRINT THE LETTER OF THE CORRECT ANSWER IN THE SPACE AT THE RIGHT.*

1. Approximately how much labor will be required for the testing of a single unit of installed water or sewer line? 1.____

   A. 30 minutes
   B. 1 hour
   C. 2 hours
   D. 3 hours

2. Concrete reinforcing bars are sized according to ______ inch increments. 2.____

   A. 1/16
   B. 1/8
   C. 1/4
   D. 1/2

3. Approximately how many square feet of 4 1/4" x 4 1/4" glazed wall tile, set in mortar, can be applied in an average work day? 3.____

   A. 60
   B. 130
   C. 175
   D. 220

4. In residential work, what type of estimate is MOST likely to be used to estimate the cost of excavation work? 4.____

   A. Quantity survey
   B. Lump-sum amount
   C. Cost-per-square-foot estimate
   D. Unit cost estimate

5. What type of brick masonry unit is represented by the drawing shown at the right? 5.____

   A. Trough
   B. Economy
   C. King Norman
   D. Engineer

6. Which of the following types of windows would be MOST expensive to install? 6.____

   A. Aluminum, single-hung vertical
   B. Wood, double-hung
   C. Steel, projected vent
   D. Aluminum, projected vent

7. For estimating the labor cost of the installation of tile base and cap units, the typical tile labor time should be multiplied by 7.____

   A. 1/2
   B. 2
   C. 3
   D. 4

8. What is represented by the architectural symbol shown at the right? 8.____

   A. Plywood
   B. Vertical paneling
   C. Brick
   D. Rough lumber

9. Approximately how long should it take a 2-person crew to install 100 linear feet of 4" x 6" girder? 9.____

A. 30 minutes
B. 1 hour
C. 3 hours
D. 1 work day

10. Each of the following is considered a fixed overhead cost EXCEPT 10.____

A. office rent
B. job site utilities
C. assembly space
D. stationery

11. How many square feet of solid plywood roof sheathing should two carpenters be able to install in a typical work day? 11.____

A. 400
B. 800
C. 1,000
D. 1,400

12. What type of concrete masonry unit is represented by the drawing shown at the right? 12.____

A. Floor
B. Bull nose
C. Trough
D. Jamb

13. Which type of paving material will generally take LONGEST to install? 13.____

A. Asphalt
B. Gravel base course
C. Concrete curb/gutter
D. Concrete sidewalk

14. If a roof needs to be framed for locations such as dormers, hips, or valleys, an estimator should calculate a reduction in output of ______%. 14.____

A. 5
B. 10
C. 20
D. 30

15. What is represented by the architectural symbol shown at the right? 15.____

A. Stone concrete
B. Cinder concrete
C. Gravel
D. Rock

16. Which of the following types of tile for resilient flooring would be MOST expensive? 16.____

A. Pure vinyl
B. Cork
C. Vinyl asbestos
D. Rubberized marbleized

17. Installation of tempered or insulated glass will cost approximately ______% more than the installation of 1/4" polished plate glass. 17.____

A. 20
B. 50
C. 75
D. 100

18. Most concrete is considered to be completely cured after a period of 18.____

A. 1 1/2 weeks
B. 28 days
C. 45 days
D. 4 months

19. What type of window is hinged at the top so that it may be opened outward at the bottom? 19.____

A. Storm
B. Casement
C. Sash
D. Awning

20. What is the usual thickness, in inches, for the finish coat in MOST plastering projects? 20.____

A. 1/16 B. 1/8 C. 1/4 D. 1/2

21. Due to the *swell factor* involved in excavation, 1 cubic yard of excavated sand or gravel may measure ______% more as waste or backfill. 21.____

A. 10 B. 20 C. 30 D. 50

22. What is represented by the electrical symbol shown at the right? 22.____

A. Blanked outlet
B. Signal push button
C. Special purpose outlet
D. Gauge

23. What type of nails are typically used for installing rafters? 23.____

A. 4d B. 8d C. 12d D. 16d

24. Most flat interior paint averages a coverage of about ______ square feet per gallon. 24.____

A. 100-150 B. 200-250 C. 300-400 D. 450-550

25. Which of the following types of doors would be MOST expensive? 25.____

A. Hollow core, birch-veneer face
B. Solid core, walnut-faced
C. Hollow core, hardboard-faced
D. Solid core, birch-veneer face

KEY (CORRECT ANSWERS)

1. C
2. B
3. A
4. D
5. D

6. B
7. B
8. D
9. C
10. B

11. D
12. D
13. C
14. B
15. A

16. A
17. D
18. B
19. D
20. B

21. B
22. C
23. D
24. C
25. B

TEST 3

DIRECTIONS: Each question or incomplete statement is followed by several suggested answers or completions. Select the one that BEST answers the question or completes the statement. *PRINT THE LETTER OF THE CORRECT ANSWER IN THE SPACE AT THE RIGHT.*

1. Most tubs, toilets, sinks, and lavatories require an average of _______ hours labor for the installation of finish plumbing. 1._____

   A. 3 B. 5 C. 7 D. 9

2. What size is most wire used for ranges and other heavy-draw equipment? 2._____

   A. 2-4 B. 5-7 C. 8-10 D. 12-16

3. A 4-man crew using hand application will typically be able to apply _______ square yards of gypsum plaster in one work day. 3._____

   A. 35-40 B. 45-60 C. 75-80 D. 85-100

4. A _______ is represented by the mechanical symbol shown at the right. 4._____

   A. lock and shield valve
   B. strainer
   C. pressure reducing valve
   D. drain line

5. What type of drywall surface is used for ceramic tile installation? 5._____

   A. Plain manila paper
   B. Chemically-treated paper
   C. Aluminum foil
   D. Greenboard

6. Which of the following steps in a grading-quantity estimation would be performed LAST? 6._____

   A. Determine approximate finish grade
   B. Calculate difference between cut and fill
   C. Estimate elevation of grid corners from contours
   D. Average the elevation of each grid square

7. In order to give desired rigidity to a wall, the top plates must overlap AT LEAST _______ inches at each joint along the wall. 7._____

   A. 12 B. 24 C. 48 D. 60

8. The horizontal framing member above window and door openings is called the 8._____

   A. molding B. footer C. chord D. lintel

9. Which of the following waterproofing materials is MOST expensive? 9._____

   A. 30-lb. asphalt paper with elastic adhesive
   B. Elastomeric waterproofing (1/32")
   C. Asphalt-coated protective board, installed in mastic
   D. Sprayed-on bituminous coating

10. If a site lawn is seeded, for how long will a contractor typically assume the responsibility for maintaining the lawn? 10._____

   A. 3 weeks B. 1 month C. 3 months D. 6 months

11. What is represented by the architectural symbol shown at the right? 11.____

A. Brick
B. Vertical paneling
C. Ceramic tile
D. Concrete block

12. In an average work day, approximately how many square feet of brick (on sand bed) paving can be laid down? 12.____

A. 80-100 B. 600 C. 1800 D. 3000-4000

13. In lumber take-off and ordering, costs are kept separate and calculated for each of the following specifications EXCEPT 13.____

A. size B. grade C. length D. species

14. The excavation of sand will require an angle of repose (slope) of 1 ft. vertical to _______ ft. horizontal. 14.____

A. 3/4 B. 1 C. 1 1/2 D. 2

15. Concrete sidewalks are typically poured to a depth of _______ inches. 15.____

A. 2 B. 4 C. 6 D. 8

16. What type of concrete masonry unit is represented by the drawing shown at the right? 16.____

A. Stretcher
B. Pier
C. Jamb
D. Beam

17. Each of the following is a factor in estimating the total cost according to a quantity survey EXCEPT 17.____

A. quantity of each material
B. square foot area of building
C. cost of labor for each unit of material
D. profit

18. Approximately how many hours will it take carpentry labor to install 100 square feet of wall space, without openings? 18.____

A. 1 B. 3 C. 5 D. 7

19. Each of the following is included in a site plan EXCEPT 19.____

A. size of property
B. legal description
C. number of external doors
D. driveways

20. What is represented by the electrical symbol shown at the right? 20.____

A. Street light and bracket
B. Call system
C. Wall bracket light fixture
D. Sound system

21. Normally, horizontal reinforcements for masonry walls are spaced about ______ inches apart. 21.____

A. 18 B. 36 C. 48 D. 60

22. Which of the following paving materials is generally LEAST expensive? 22.____

A. Brick on sand bed
B. Random flagstone
C. Asphalt
D. Concrete

23. What type of nails are typically used for installing shingles? 23.____

A. 4d B. 8d C. 12d D. 16d

24. A miter joint is cut at a ______ ° angle. 24.____

A. 30 B. 45 C. 60 D. 90

25. Generally, ceiling joists must be braced if the distance between supports is greater than 25.____

A. 18 inches B. 24 inches C. 4 feet D. 8 feet

KEY (CORRECT ANSWERS)

1. A
2. C
3. C
4. A
5. B

6. B
7. C
8. D
9. C
10. C

11. B
12. A
13. C
14. D
15. B

16. B
17. B
18. B
19. C
20. A

21. C
22. C
23. A
24. B
25. D

EXAMINATION SECTION
TEST 1

DIRECTIONS: Each question or incomplete statement is followed by several suggested answers or completions. Select the one that BEST answers the question or completes the statement. *PRINT THE LETTER OF THE CORRECT ANSWER IN THE SPACE AT THE RIGHT.*

1. What is the term for the single wood member laid on top of the foundation wall? 1.____

   A. Soffit B. Primer C. Jack D. Sill

2. What is represented by the mechanical symbol shown at the right? 2.____

   A. Gauge B. 45° elbow
   C. Shower head D. Lavatory or sink

3. What is generally considered to be the MINIMUM roof pitch allowable for the use of shingles and shakes? 3.____
   ______ in 12.

   A. 1 B. 2 C. 3 D. 4

4. Approximately how many square feet of drywall can be hung by a single installer in an average work day? 4.____

   A. 200 B. 450 C. 800 D. 1150

5. Normally, the length of a nail is designated as 5.____

   A. casing B. gauge C. chase D. penny

6. Approximately how many pounds of prepared drywall taping compound, or *mud,* will be required for 1000 square feet of area? 6.____

   A. 25 B. 50 C. 75 D. 100

7. What is represented by the architectural symbol shown at the right? 7.____

   A. Stone concrete B. Cinder concrete
   C. Gravel D. Rock

8. Which of the following constructions is NOT typically found in kitchen sinks? 8.____

   A. Enameled pressed steel B. Enameled cast iron
   C. Cast ceramic D. Stainless steel

9. The Uniform System separates construction specifications into ______ divisions. 9.____

   A. 4 B. 7 C. 11 D. 16

10. Which of the following structures typically requires lumber that has been pressure-treated? 10.____

    A. Mud sill B. Joist C. Stud D. Rafter

11. If boards, rather than plywood, are used as the contact surface for foundation forms, how much of the board material should be calculated as waste? 11.____

A. 5% B. 15% C. 25% D. 40%

12. What is the term for the lateral bracing of floor joists? 12.____

A. Crippling B. Coursing C. Fitting D. Bridging

13. Approximately how many pounds of 8d nails will be required to install 1,000 board-feet of roof sheathing? 13.____

A. 10 B. 25 C. 40 D. 65

14. What is represented by the electrical symbol shown at the right? 14.____

A. Wiring in floor
B. Circuit breaker
C. Conduit with wires
D. Switch and pilot light

15. Approximately how long will it take a two-person team to install a 10' length of 4" plastic soil line? 15.____

A. 15 minutes
B. 30 minutes
C. 1 hour
D. 1 1/2 hours

16. If forms are to be used for a foundation, the exterior face of the excavation should be made _______ inches beyond the wall line of the foundation. 16.____

A. 6 B. 12 C. 18 D. 32

17. What is the MOST commonly used type of roll roofing material? 17.____

A. Smooth
B. Saturated felt
C. Selvage edged
D. Mineral surfaced

18. Approximately how many pounds of oakum are required per joint in one sewer line lead-and-oakum seal? 18.____

A. 1/4 B. 1/2 C. 1 1/2 D. 3

19. What is the term for the construction beneath a foundation, usually of concrete, which helps distribute the imposed loads? 19.____

A. Gasket
B. Footing
C. Escutcheon
D. Sill

20. Approximately how many hours of labor are required for the installation of a single check valve in a length of water pipe? 20.____

A. 1/4-1/2 B. 3/4-1 1/2 C. 1-3 D. 2-4

21. In an average work day, how many cubic yards of earth can be excavated by means of a backhoe? 21.____

A. 10 B. 75 C. 125 D. 350

22. A _______ line is represented by the mechanical symbol shown at the right? ▬ ▬ ▬ ▬ ▬ 22._____

    A. compressed air B. sprinkler main
    C. cold water D. vent

23. How many floor joists would be required for a 20-foot-long span of flooring? 23._____

    A. 10 B. 15 C. 16 D. 20

24. Of the following, bathroom tubs are MOST commonly made of 24._____

    A. enameled cast iron
    B. enameled pressed steel
    C. glazed cast ceramic
    D. enameled stainless steel

25. When calculating the air conditioning needs for a building, a loss factor of _______ should be used for the exposure of walls to the exterior on all sides. 25._____

    A. 2.0 B. 3.5 C. 6.0 D. 7.5

KEY (CORRECT ANSWERS)

1. D
2. A
3. C
4. C
5. D

6. C
7. D
8. C
9. D
10. A

11. B
12. D
13. C
14. B
15. C

16. C
17. D
18. A
19. B
20. B

21. B
22. D
23. C
24. A
25. C

TEST 2

DIRECTIONS: Each question or incomplete statement is followed by several suggested answers or completions. Select the one that BEST answers the question or completes the statement. *PRINT THE LETTER OF THE CORRECT ANSWER IN THE SPACE AT THE RIGHT.*

1. Which of the following are typically drawn to a larger scale than architectural plans? 1.____

   A. Diagrams B. Sections C. Details D. Elevations

2. About how many door/window openings should a workman be able to caulk or seal in an average work day? 2.____

   A. 10 B. 20 C. 30 D. 40

3. The typical residential air conditioning requirement per 1 square foot of space is about ______ British Thermal Units (BTU's). 3.____

   A. 20 B. 30 C. 40 D. 50

4. What is represented by the mechanical symbol shown at the right? 4.____ 
   A. Automatic expansion valve
   B. Gauge
   C. Compressor
   D. Water closet, tank type

5. In an average work day, approximately how many cubic yards of earth can be excavated by means of crew hand shoveling and truck loading? 5.____

   A. 3-7 B. 8-10 C. 12-27 D. 18-32

6. The labor for installation of bath accessories should be calculated as 6.____

   A. plumbing B. tile
   C. common labor D. carpentry

7. Which of the following materials, purchased for gutters, would be LEAST expensive? 7.____

   A. Zinc alloy B. Galvanized steel
   C. Copper D. Zinc

8. Which of the following is NOT classified as *rough* electrical work? 8.____

   A. Conduit and wiring
   B. Installation of service equipment
   C. Switch and outlet boxes
   D. Connections to motors and fans

9. Approximately how many square feet of interior acoustic duct lining can be installed in an average work day? 9.____

   A. 25-50 B. 50-75 C. 75-120 D. 100-125

10. The *R-value* of insulation material is a function of each of the following characteristics EXCEPT 10.____

A. thickness B. height
C. vapor barrier D. air space

11. Generally, finishing hardware costs will be a MINIMUM of ______% of the total job cost. 11.____

A. .5 B. 1 C. 3 D. 7

12. Due to the *swell factor* involved in excavation, 1 cubic yard of excavated rock may measure ______% more as waste or backfill. 12.____

A. 10 B. 20 C. 30 D. 50

13. What type of concrete masonry unit is represented by the drawing shown at the right? 13.____

A. Partition
B. Floor
C. Trough
D. Frogged brick

14. Which of the following wood floor materials would be LEAST expensive to install? 14.____

A. Unfinished plank B. Walnut parquet
C. Maple strip D. Oak parquet

15. What is generally considered to be the MAXIMUM roof pitch allowable for the use of mineral-surfaced roll roofing? ______ in 12. 15.____

A. 1 B. 2 C. 3 D. 4

16. Most stains that are applied to interior wood finish can cover about ______ square feet per gallon. 16.____

A. 100 B. 250 C. 350 D. 550

17. The exposed finishing hardware on windows is USUALLY made of 17.____

A. steel B. aluminum C. wood D. bronze

18. What would the calculated BM (board measure) be for a length of lumber measuring 2" x 12" x 10"? 18.____

A. 10 B. 20 C. 48 D. 240

19. Which of the following materials, purchased as sheet metal flashing for roofing, would be LEAST expensive? 19.____

A. Aluminum B. Galvanized steel
C. Copper D. Zinc

20. Approximately how long will it take one worker to complete the lathing work for 100 square feet of a non-bearing wall? 20.____

A. 30 minutes B. 1 hour
C. 90 minutes D. Two hours

21. Sewer pipe is MOST often made of 21.____

A. plastic
B. copper
C. galvanized steel
D. cast iron

22. In an average work day, approximately how many cubic yards of earth can be backfilled by means of a man-operated pneumatic tamper? 22.____

A. 8-10
B. 12-20
C. 30-40
D. 75

23. A _______ is used to calculate the total cost of electrical work. 23.____

A. quantity survey
B. lump-sum amount
C. cost-per-square-foot estimate
D. unit cost estimate

24. What is represented by the architectural symbol shown at the right? 24.____

A. Plywood
B. Wood finish
C. Rough lumber
D. Vertical paneling

25. For how many hours should a *C label* fire door be able to withstand continuous fire exposure? 25.____

A. 3/4
B. 1
C. 1 1/2
D. 3

KEY (CORRECT ANSWERS)

1.	B	11.	A
2.	C	12.	D
3.	A	13.	D
4.	C	14.	C
5.	B	15.	A
6.	D	16.	D
7.	B	17.	D
8.	D	18.	B
9.	D	19.	A
10.	B	20.	D

21. D
22. C
23. A
24. A
25. A

TEST 3

DIRECTIONS: Each question or incomplete statement is followed by several suggested answers or completions. Select the one that BEST answers the question or completes the statement. *PRINT THE LETTER OF THE CORRECT ANSWER IN THE SPACE AT THE RIGHT.*

1. Exterior paints are commonly made from all of the following materials EXCEPT 1.____

   A. alkyd resin B. oleoresin
   C. full latex D. oil latex

2. Due to the *swell factor* involved in excavation, 1 cubic yard of excavated *normal* earth may measure ______% more as waste or backfill. 2.____

   A. 10 B. 20 C. 30 D. 50

3. According to established finish-designation standards, which of the following finish materials would be ranked at the LOWEST grade? 3.____

   A. White bronze B. Bright bronze
   C. Sanded dull black D. Cadmium-plated

4. Which plumbing component takes waste from a building to the municipal sewer? 4.____

   A. Drain line B. Soil line
   C. Clean-out D. Trap

5. Approximately how many pounds of 6d nails will be required to install 1000 square feet of siding? 5.____

   A. 10-12 B. 15-17 C. 35-40 D. 45-50

6. Calculations for paving amounts are typically made in units of 6.____

   A. surface square feet B. surface linear feet
   C. cubic feet D. weight

7. Which of the following types of glass will be MOST expensive? 7.____

   A. 1/4"clear plate
   B. 1/8" patterned *obscure* glass
   C. 1/4" tempered plate
   D. 1/4" wire glass

8. What type of brick masonry unit is represented by the drawing shown at the right? 8.____

   A. Modular
   B. Norwegian
   C. Roman
   D. Engineer

   2
   12
   4

9. Approximately how many pounds of flooring nails are required for the installation of 1000 square feet of wood strip flooring? 9.____

   A. 10 B. 25 C. 35 D. 50

10. The cost for masonry work is typically estimated in terms of 10.____

A. surface square feet
B. surface linear feet
C. cubic feet
D. weight

11. In most newer buildings, vent piping is made of 11.____

A. galvanized steel
B. lead
C. cast iron
D. plastic

12. If 2" x 10" ceiling joists are installed with 16" of space between them, approximately how many hours of labor will it take to install joists for 100 square feet of ceiling area? 12.____

A. 1 1/2
B. 3 1/2
C. 5 1/2
D. 7 1/2

13. What type of labor will usually be responsible for the installation of fiberglass batten insulation? 13.____

A. Finish
B. Roofing
C. Common labor
D. Carpentry

14. What is generally considered to be the MINIMUM allowable pitch of a roof that will be furnished with standing seam? 14.____
______ in 12.

A. 2
B. 3
C. 4
D. 5

15. A ______ valve is represented by the mechanical symbol shown at the right? 15.____

A. diaphragm
B. lock and shield
C. gate
D. check

16. Approximately how many linear feet of galvanized steel pipe can be installed in a typical work day? 16.____

A. 35-40
B. 50-60
C. 65-75
D. 85-100

17. Reinforcement anchor bolts are typically spaced around a building at ______ intervals. 17.____

A. 4"-6"
B. 8"-12"
C. 1'-4'
D. 4'-6'

18. Which of the following types of wall constructions will have the GREATEST sound-dampening effect? 18.____

A. Single-stud gypsum board
B. Metal-stud plaster on lath
C. Single-stud plaster on gypsum board
D. Staggered-stud gypsum board

19. For accurate painting estimates for wall openings, such as doors and windows, the general practice is to add ______ to all height and width figures associated with the openings. 19.____

A. 6 inches
B. 1 foot
C. 2 feet
D. 4 feet

20. In an average work day, approximately how many square feet of rock or gravel base course for paving can be laid down? 20.____

A. 80-100 B. 600 C. 1800 D. 3000-4000

21. Each of the following is a factor in the estimation of door costs EXCEPT 21.____
    A. size B. lockset C. type D. finish

22. What is represented by the mechanical symbol shown at the right? 22.____
    A. Automatic expansion valve
    B. Ceiling air outlet
    C. Floor drain
    D. Reducer

23. Concrete for on-grade floor installations should typically have a compressive strength of AT LEAST ______ psi. 23.____
    A. 500 B. 1000 C. 1500 D. 2000

24. Bathroom toilets are MOST commonly made of 24.____
    A. enameled cast iron
    B. enameled pressed steel
    C. glazed cast ceramic
    D. enameled stainless steel

25. Which of the following types of windows would be LEAST expensive to install? 25.____
    A. Aluminum, horizontal sliding
    B. Wood, casement
    C. Steel, double-hung
    D. Aluminum, projected vent

KEY (CORRECT ANSWERS)

1. B
2. C
3. D
4. B
5. A
6. A
7. C
8. C
9. D
10. A
11. D
12. B
13. D
14. B
15. D
16. C
17. D
18. D
19. C
20. D
21. B
22. A
23. D
24. C
25. A

EXAMINATION SECTION
TEST 1

DIRECTIONS: Each question or incomplete statement is followed by several suggested answers or completions. Select the one that BEST answers the question or completes the statement. *PRINT THE LETTER OF THE CORRECT ANSWER IN THE SPACE AT THE RIGHT.*

1. The specifications for a construction job state that the bench top of a table shall be made of 1/2-inch transite. Transite is a(n) 1._____

   A. thermo-setting plastic B. titanium steel alloy
   C. gypsum-cement product D. asbestos-cement product

2. High early-strength cement is designated as Type 2._____

   A. I B. II C. III D. IV

3. The average weight of stone concrete is MOST NEARLY ______ lbs./cu.ft. 3._____

   A. 100 B. 150 C. 200 D. 250

4. Concrete mixes made with lightweight aggregate USUALLY require the addition of an air-entraining agent in order to 4._____

   A. reduce the weight of the concrete
   B. make the concrete more workable
   C. make the concrete more waterproof
   D. reduce the setting time of the concrete

5. The addition of lime to cement mortar improves the workability of the mortar and 5._____

   A. *decreases* the setting time
   B. *increases* the water tightness
   C. *increases* the strength
   D. *decreases* the shrinkage

6. A mortar joint in a brick wall in which the joint is made flush with the brick is called a ______ joint. 6._____

   A. cut B. weather C. painted D. stripped

7. Quarry tile is made of 7._____

   A. marble B. cement and sand
   C. clay D. limestone

8. The base composition of *drywall* is 8._____

   A. vermiculite B. perlite
   C. gypsum D. Portland cement

9. The specifications for a construction job state: Furnish and erect chair rail of birch with continuous kerfing where required by room finish schedule.
   Kerfing means MOST NEARLY 9._____

   A. planing B. rounding C. jointing D. grooving

10. Cement that has become lumpy after being stored on a job site may 10.____

    A. be used anywhere if screened
    B. be used only for foundations
    C. not be used at all
    D. be used anywhere if dried out thoroughly

11. The BEST of the following sources of information to use to obtain information concerning the product of a particular manufacturer of flooring is 11.____

    A. Sweet's Catalog
    B. Architectural Standards
    C. The Flooring Institute
    D. The ASTM

12. In masonry work, a bull nose brick would be located 12.____

    A. at the inside corner of a wall
    B. at an outside corner of a wall
    C. on the inside of a boiler flue
    D. in the key of an arch

13. The thickness of double-strength glass (D.S.) is MOST NEARLY 13.____

    A. 1/8" B. 3/16" C. 1/4" D. 5/16"

14. Of the following types of paint, the one that can MOST readily be applied by spraying is 14.____

    A. lacquer
    B. shellac
    C. varnish
    D. bituminous-based paints

15. Of the following, the designation that would apply to brick is 15.____

    A. Grade A
    B. Grade SW
    C. Select Quality
    D. No. 1 Common

16. The size of the hole that is punched in structural steel to accommodate a 3/4-inch rivet should be _______ inch. 16.____

    A. 3/4 B. 13/16 C. 7/8 D. 15/16

17. In lightweight concrete, the lightweight material is substituted PRIMARILY for 17.____

    A. water B. sand C. cement D. gravel

18. The thickness of a sheet of 16-ounce copper is MOST NEARLY _______ inch. 18.____

    A. 1/50 B. 1/30 C. 1/20 D. 1/8

19. One cubic foot of dry sand weighs MOST NEARLY _______ lbs. 19.____

    A. 70 B. 94 C. 110 D. 150

20. The main difference between plate glass and sheet glass is that plate glass 20.____

    A. has a better surface finish than sheet glass
    B. absorbs heat better than sheet glass
    C. is tempered, while sheet glass is not
    D. is thinner than sheet glass

21. Stainless steel (18-8) contains 18% ______ nickel and 8% ______. 21.____

A. nickel; zinc
B. nickel; chromium
C. zinc; nickel
D. zinc; chromium

22. The specifications for a construction job state: The subframe shall be formed 1/4" thick aluminum bar with corners mitered. 22.____
Which of the following is so formed?

A.  B. 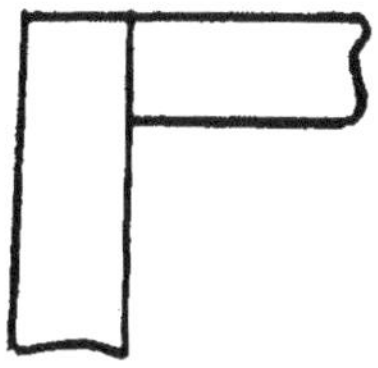 C. 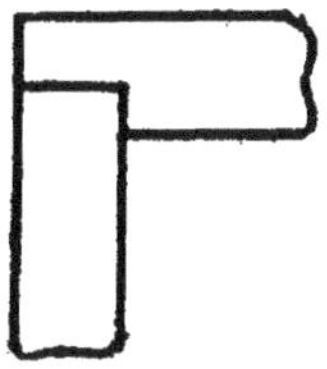 D.

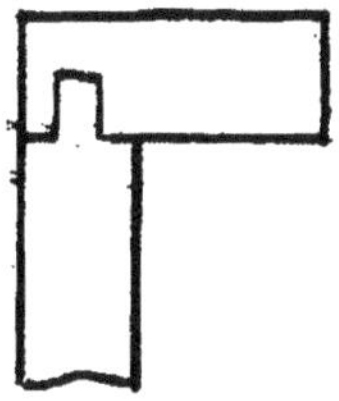

23. The coarse aggregate used in making terrazzo floors is MOST usually chips of 23.____

A. limestone
B. granite
C. brick
D. marble

24. Projected sash are 24.____

A. windows that open inward or outward
B. double hung windows
C. storm windows
D. fixed picture windows

25. For a school building, the number of reinforcing bars in a slab would be indicated on the 25.____

A. architectural plans
B. structural engineer's plans
C. reinforcing steel shop drawings
D. standard detail drawings

KEY (CORRECT ANSWERS)

1. D
2. C
3. B
4. B
5. D

6. A
7. C
8. C
9. D
10. C

11. A
12. B
13. A
14. A
15. B

16. B
17. D
18. A
19. C
20. A

21. B
22. A
23. D
24. A
25. C

TEST 2

DIRECTIONS: Each question or incomplete statement is followed by several suggested answers or completions. Select the one that BEST answers the question or completes the statement. *PRINT THE LETTER OF THE CORRECT ANSWER IN THE SPACE AT THE RIGHT.*

1. The ADVANTAGES of gypsum mortar over lime mortar for use in plaster work are that gypsum mortar is stronger and ______ than lime mortar. 1.____

   A. is more compact
   B. sets more quickly
   C. works more easily
   D. contains more entrained air

2. In concrete work, a dummy joint is MOST similar in purpose to a(n) ______ joint. 2.____

   A. construction B. expansion
   C. contraction D. shear

3. In the welding symbol, 3/8 ◺ 2-5, the 2 represents the 3.____

   A. length of the individual weld, in inches
   B. spacing between the welds, in inches
   C. number of sides to be welded
   D. thickness of the throat of the weld, in eighths of an inch

4. Where vinyl tile is to be laid directly upon a concrete floor, the finish on the concrete surface should be 4.____

   A. wood floated B. broomed
   C. steel trowelled D. darbied

5. Specifications for hollow metal doors to be used on a construction job state: Double door without mullions; spot weld astragal to inactive door. 5.____
   Astragal, as used in the above statement, means MOST NEARLY

   A. louver B. hinge C. molding D. veneer

6. The concrete surface of a reinforced concrete building is 1/4 inch below the finished floor. Of the following, the floor finish MOST likely to be installed is 6.____

   A. wood flooring B. ceramic tile
   C. asphalt tile D. terrazzo

7. Of the following, aluminum castings are USUALLY made from alloy 7.____

   A. 43 B. 3003 C. 1100 D. 6063

8. Specifications for a building state that reinforcing bars must lap 40 diameters in the concrete. 8.____
   The length of lap for a number 5 bar should be

   A. 15" B. 25" C. 30" D. 35"

9. The MAXIMUM size fillet weld that can usually be made in a single pass for other than vertical welds in ordinary structural steel work is _______ inch. 9._____

A. 3/16 B. 5/16 C. 7/16 D. 9/16

10. The specifications for a construction job state: The contractor shall make additional borings at locations directed by the executive director, for which he will receive additional payment at the rate of $6.00 per lineal foot for earth borings, and $7.50 per lineal foot for rock borings. In addition to rate per lineal foot for borings, the contractor will be paid an additional sum of money in the amount of $150.00 to defray the cost of transporting drilling equipment to the site, setting up the equipment, dismantling same, and transporting equipment away from the site after completion of the work. If an additional boring is ordered that is through 40 feet of earth and 5 feet of rock, the contractor would be entitled to 10._____

A. $187.50 B. $277.50 C. $390.00 D. $427.50

11. The specifications for a construction job state: Cement content shall not exceed 7 1/2 sacks nor be less than 6 sacks per cubic yard of concrete. 11._____
The ratio of the number of sacks of cement per cubic yard of concrete is known as the

A. water-cement ratio
B. yield
C. ultimate strength
D. cement factor

12. The specifications for a construction job state that the deflection of the facing materials between the studs as well as the deflection of the studs shall be limited to .0025 times the span. 12._____
If the span is 8 1/4", the MAXIMUM allowable deflection is _______ inch.

A. 1/8 B. 1/4 C. 3/8 D. 1/2

13. The specifications for a construction job state that job chutes for placing concrete shall have a slope of not more than one vertical to two horizontal and not less than one vertical to three horizontal. 13._____
If the horizontal distance of the run of chute is 20 feet, a difference in elevation between the start and the end of the chute that is acceptable is _______ feet.

A. 6 B. 9 C. 12 D. 15

14. The specifications relating to cavity wall brick construction state: In laying up face brick, the mason shall leave temporary openings (one brick) approximately five feet on centers and at all internal and external corners in the first course of brick above the foundation wall and in brick courses resting on angle lintels. 14._____
The purpose of these temporary openings is to allow for

A. expansion or contraction
B. the erection of scaffolds
C. cleaning off the wall flashings
D. draining off water that may get into the wall cavity

15. Of the following size electrodes for ordinary structural steel welding, the one that would MOST likely be used for vertical and overhead welding is _______ inch. 15._____

A. 1/16 B. 3/16 C. 5/16 D. 7/16

16. The number of anchor bolts used to anchor a steel column to a footing is USUALLY 16.____

A. 1 B. 2 C. 3 D. 4

17. Specifications for precasting for a construction job state: Dimensions shall be within a tolerance of plus 0 to minus 3/32. 17.____
If the specified dimension is 24 inches, the one of the following actual dimensions which would be UNACCEPTABLE is ______ inches.

A. 24-1/32 B. 24 C. 23-31/32 D. 23-15/16

18. Of the following, the one that would be the composition of grout under a billet plate is 18.____

A. neat cement
B. 1 part cement, 2 parts sand
C. 1 part cement, 2 parts sand, 3 parts gravel
D. 1 part cement, 1 part lime, 2 parts sand

19. Specifications for concrete for a construction job state that slab forms shall be set with a camber of 1/4 inch per 10 feet of slab. 19.____
Of the following, the BEST reason for providing camber in the forms is to

A. allow for adjustment during pouring
B. prevent overloading of the wood forms during pouring
C. allow for drainage before pouring
D. eliminate sag in the finishing slab

20. Specifications for concrete construction state that the contractor must provide for rebates, reglets, keys, and chamfers. 20.____
Rebates are

A. grooves B. grounds C. chases D. ties

21. Concrete driveways built across sidewalks must have a MINIMUM thickness of ______ inches. 21.____

A. 4 B. 6 C. 7 D. 8

22. Wire mesh is designated 4 x 16 - 3/8. 22.____
The *16* represents the ______ of the wires.

A. spacing; longitudinal B. spacing; transverse
C. size; longitudinal D. size; transverse

23. Specifications for a construction job state: Install 6 mil carbon vinyl membrane. 23.____
The *6 mil* means 6

A. millimeters B. thousandths of an inch
C. hundredths of an inch D. tenths of an inch

24. It is poor practice to use a vibrator to move newly poured concrete into place. 24.____
Of the following, the BEST reason for not using a vibrator for this purpose is to prevent

A. air entrapment in the concrete
B. segregation of the aggregates
C. premature setting of the concrete
D. premature drying out of the surface of the concrete

25. Expanded slag, shale, or clay would weigh MOST NEARLY _____ pounds per cubic foot. 25.____

A. 30 B. 90 C. 150 D. 210

KEY (CORRECT ANSWERS)

1. B
2. C
3. A
4. C
5. C

6. C
7. A
8. B
9. B
10. D

11. D
12. B
13. B
14. C
15. B

16. B
17. A
18. B
19. D
20. A

21. C
22. B
23. B
24. B
25. B

EXAMINATION SECTION
TEST 1

DIRECTIONS: Each question or incomplete statement is followed by several suggested answers or completions. Select the one that BEST answers the question or completes the statement. *PRINT THE LETTER OF THE CORRECT ANSWER IN THE SPACE AT THE RIGHT.*

1. Of the following aggregates, the one LEAST frequently used in the manufacture of light-weight concrete is 1.____

   A. cinders B. slag C. perlite D. mica

2. The purpose of a chase is to 2.____

   A. accommodate pipes in a wall
   B. act as a support for a stair stringer
   C. provide clearance between wood frame and a chimney
   D. flash block into a parapet

3. In masonry work, a bullnose brick would be used at 3.____

   A. an inside corner
   B. an outside corner
   C. the key of an arch
   D. the roof of a boiler setting

4. When asphalt shingles are applied to a sloping roof, a cant strip is frequently used. The purpose of this cant strip is to 4.____

   A. prevent leaking at the ridge
   B. hold together opposite sides of a valley
   C. eliminate the possibility of wind lifting the shingles
   D. raise the lower edge of the first course of shingles

5. Air entrained concrete is used rather than ordinary concrete MAINLY to provide additional resistance to 5.____

   A. fire B. impact
   C. freezing and thawing D. water penetration

6. The type of construction MOST commonly used in new wood frame dwellings is the ______ frame. 6.____

   A. platform B. braced C. balloon D. butt

7. Of the following, the one LEAST commonly used for flashing is 7.____

   A. copper B. monel
   C. polyethylene D. asphalt felt

8. The end of a wood joist resting directly on a concrete wall has to be brought up to level. The BEST material to use as a shim for this purpose is 8.____

   A. slate B. wood shingles
   C. dressed wood D. grout

9. In foundation work, an example of a rock that would be considered a SOFT rock is 9.____

A. gneiss B. granite C. shale D. limestone

10. Segregation in concrete will result from improper 10.____

A. curing B. placing C. formwork D. finishing

11. One method of dewatering an excavation for a foundation is the use of 11.____

A. inverted siphons
B. line holes
C. well points
D. suction heads

12. An excavation for a concrete footing to support a steel column was accidentally dug 4" too deep. 12.____
Of the following, the BEST practice would be to

A. make the footing 4" thicker
B. backfill the 4" with stone
C. backfill the 4" with clean sand and puddle the fill carefully
D. lower the footing 4"

13. The MOST common finish for a concrete walk is a ______ finish. 13.____

A. steel trowel
B. screeded
C. sealed
D. wood float

14. In setting diagonal cross bridging on wood joists, the BEST method is to 14.____

A. nail at top and bottom before subflooring is in place
B. nail at bottom, place subflooring, then nail at top
C. nail at top, place subflooring, then nail at bottom
D. place subflooring, then nail at top and bottom

15. In a fireproof building, purlins used to support a suspended ceiling are USUALLY 15.____

A. T B. channel C. I D. lattice

16. *Standing seams* are MOST frequently found in ______ roofs. 16.____

A. built up
B. poured gypsum
C. copper
D. concrete plank

17. Long span steel floor joists differ from ordinary light steel beams used as joists in that the long span joists 17.____

A. come with welded plank clips on the top flange
B. do not require fireproofing
C. have lower flanges with adaptors for suspended ceilings
D. have open diagonal lacing rather than solid webs

18. In fireproofing steel girders (4 hour fire rating), the minimum thickness of concrete (ordinary concrete made with trap rock) required to protect the girder is 18.____

A. 1" B. 2" C. 3" D. 4"

19. The base composition of plaster boards is 19.____

A. cement B. vermiculite
C. gypsum D. perlite

20. In the ordinary cantilever type retaining wall, the main steel reinforcing in the upright part will be ______ and nearest the side of the wall ______ the earth. 20.____

A. vertical; next to B. horizontal; next to
C. vertical; away from D. horizontal; away from

21. A major disadvantage in the use of lime mortar for brickwork is that the lime 21.____

A. sets too slowly
B. is too difficult to apply
C. discolors the brick too much
D. reduces the fire resistance of the masonry

22. Mortar joints in old brick walls are BEST repaired by 22.____

A. setting B. framing C. taping D. pointing

23. Of the following, the MAIN advantage of a 10" brick cavity wall over an 8" solid brick wall is that the cavity wall 23.____

A. is stronger
B. resists rain penetration better
C. is not affected by freezing and thawing
D. can be used with more varieties of bond

24. In large metropolitan cities, masonry structural units are considered *solid* structural units when they are (select SMALLEST acceptable value) ______ *solid.* 24.____

A. 70% B. 75% C. 80% D. 85%

25. The PRIMARY function of a vapor barrier is to 25.____

A. stop water from entering the space between a parapet wall and a roof surface
B. prevent a driving rain from penetrating a roof surface
C. seal openings around a hot water pipe in a wall
D. block moisture in warm air from entering unheated ceiling and wall spaces

KEY (CORRECT ANSWERS)

1. D
2. A
3. B
4. D
5. C
6. A
7. B
8. A
9. C
10. B
11. C
12. A
13. D
14. C
15. B
16. C
17. D
18. B
19. C
20. A
21. A
22. D
23. B
24. B
25. D

TEST 2

DIRECTIONS: Each question or incomplete statement is followed by several suggested answers or completions. Select the one that BEST answers the question or completes the statement. *PRINT THE LETTER OF THE CORRECT ANSWER IN THE SPACE AT THE RIGHT.*

1. On a plan, the symbol represents 1.____

   A. brick
   B. cinder concrete block
   C. hollow clay tile
   D. gypsum block

2. Where a continuous concrete floor slab is supported on concrete beams and girders, poured integrally, the BEST place to make a construction joint is at a point 2.____

   A. midway between the beams
   B. directly over the center of a beam
   C. a distance from the face of the beam equal to the depth of the beam
   D. one-third of the distance from the face of the beam to the center of the beam

3. If legal curb grade is at elevation 134.27, and the first floor level is 4'2 1/4" above legal curb grade, then the elevation of the first floor is MOST NEARLY 3.____

   A. 138.40
   B. 138.42
   C. 138.44
   D. 138.46

4. Of the following practices, the one that is MOST likely to result in segregation in concrete is 4.____

   A. inadequate floating
   B. vibrating mixes that can be readily consolidated by hand
   C. placing the chutes in such a way that the discharge end is always at the end of the fresh concrete surface
   D. placing the concrete in thin layers over the entire area to be concreted

5. Stone sills frequently have a groove cut into the underside. This is done MAINLY to 5.____

   A. assist in anchoring the sill with clips
   B. allow flashing to be inserted
   C. give the mortar a *key* or grip
   D. prevent rain dripping onto the wall

6. A permit to store paint in quantities greater than 20 gallons must be obtained from the 6.____

   A. Police Department
   B. Department of Air Resources
   C. Fire Department
   D. Building Department

7. The specifications state that glass shall have a thickness of 1/8" 1/32". Of the following thicknesses of glass, the one that does NOT meet the above specification is 7.____

   A. .090"
   B. .110"
   C. .130"
   D. .150"

8. Of the following, the one that designates a quality of clear glass is 8.____

A. Class II
B. B
C. select grade
D. transparent

9. A section of the specifications calls for concrete fill. This concrete is MOST likely to be _______ concrete. 9.____

A. reinforced
B. high early strength
C. cinder
D. sulfate resisting

10. When concrete is to have a rubbed finish, 10.____

A. the concrete must be thoroughly dry before the rubbing operation commences
B. mortar is usually used in the rubbing operation
C. grout is usually used in the rubbing operation
D. the surfaces should be kept thoroughly wet during rubbing operations

11. The specification for Average *A* concrete is as follows: 11.____

A. 1:1:3
B. 1:2:3 1/2
C. 1:2:4
D. 1:1 1/2:3

12. The specification states: *The value of each change order shall be computed separately by cost of labor and materials, plus equipment allowance, plus overhead and profit.* 12.____

The MOST probable value of overhead and profit is _______ of the cost of labor and materials plus equipment allowance.

A. 5%
B. 15%
C. 34%
D. 55%

13. In the specifications is an item, *Equipment Allowance: Shall include rental of necessary equipment plus 9% of this rental.* 13.____
According to the above specification, if a piece of equipment rents for $35 per day, Equipment Allowance for this equipment rented for 11 days is MOST NEARLY

A. $484.00
B. $378.42
C. $385.00
D. $419.65

14. Plank clips that are .062 inches thick are MOST NEARLY _______ thick. 14.____

A. 1/32"
B. 2/32"
C. 3/32"
D. 4/32"

15. Of the following types of structured steel shapes, the one of the following that is UNLIKE the others in general is 15.____

A. WF
B. H
C. I
D. T

16. Terra cotta is composed primarily of 16.____

A. limestone
B. portland cement
C. gypsum
D. clay

17. In the specification for brickwork is a paragraph entitled *bond.* 17.____
With reference to brickwork, bond refers to

A. the pattern of the brickwork
B. the guarantee of the life of the brick

C. the mortar joining the brick
D. water tightness of the brick wall

18. The specifications for the laying of block state that the joint shall be slightly concave. This would appear MOST likely as in 18.____

A. 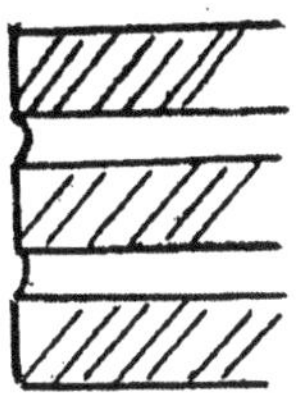 B. 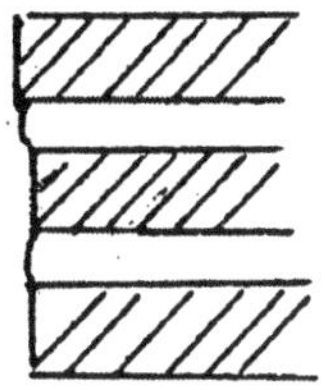 C. 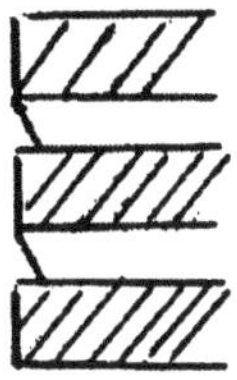 D.

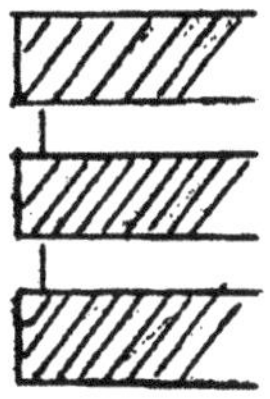

19. The maximum size of a sand particle beyond which it is NOT considered sand is _______ inch. 19.____

A. 1/16 B. 1/8 C. 3/16 D. 1/4

20. The specifications state that concrete shall have an ultimate compressive strength of 4000 psi. This means the compressive strength at the end of _______ days. 20.____

A. 7 B. 14 C. 21 D. 28

21. The primary purpose of curing a freshly poured concrete slab is to _______ the concrete. 21.____

A. prevent loss of water from
B. minimize segregation in
C. minimize honeycombing in
D. prevent efflorescense in

22. Silicone water repellent would MOST likely be used on 22.____

A. the inside of a foundation wall
B. the outside of a foundation wall
C. an exposed brick wall
D. the roof of a building

23. *Parging* of a brick wall is also known as 23.____

A. buttering
B. backplastering
C. slushing
D. scratching

24. The specifications require 2.2 lbs. metal lath. The 2.2 lbs. represents the weight per 24.____

A. foot
B. yard
C. square foot
D. square yard

25. Cleaning of glazed surfaces of a completed structural facing tile surface is BEST done by 25.____

A. sandblasting
B. washing with soap powder in boiling water
C. wire brushing
D. scrubbing with a medium solution of muriatic acid

KEY (CORRECT ANSWERS)

1. B
2. A
3. D
4. B
5. D

6. C
7. A
8. B
9. C
10. D

11. C
12. B
13. D
14. B
15. D

16. D
17. A
18. A
19. D
20. D

21. A
22. C
23. B
24. D
25. B

TEST 3

DIRECTIONS: Each question or incomplete statement is followed by several suggested answers or completions. Select the one that BEST answers the question or completes the statement. *PRINT THE LETTER OF THE CORRECT ANSWER IN THE SPACE AT THE RIGHT.*

1. A metal support for plaster is 1 1/4" x 1/2" x 1/8". The 1/2" refers to 1.____

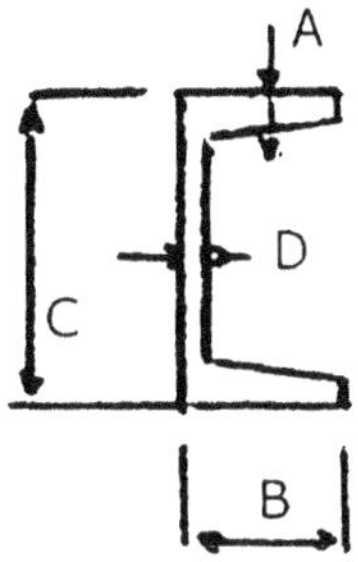

A
D
C
B

   A. A
   B. B
   C. C
   D. D

2. The specification requires stove bolts. 2.____
   The head of a stove bolt would MOST LIKELY appear as in

   A.  B.  C.  D.

3. In a hung plaster ceiling, the metal lath is tied to the 3.____

   A. runner
   B. hanger
   C. tee insert
   D. cross furring

4. Plastering has just been completed in a room. 4.____
   The proper way to ventilate the room to dry out the plaster when the outside weather conditions are moderate is to

   A. keep the window shut
   B. open the bottom window all the way
   C. open the top and bottom window 2 inches
   D. open the top window all the way

5. The specification for a wood door states: *Stiles and rails of doors M & T together and assembled with hardwood wedges.* 5.____
   M & T stands for

   A. mitred and tongued
   B. matches and tacked
   C. milled and tacked
   D. mortise and tenon

6. The weight of a gallon of ordinary paint, in pounds, is MOST NEARLY 6.____

   A. 5 B. 13 C. 21 D. 29

7. A section in the specification is entitled *Resilient Flooring.* 7.____
   Of the following types of flooring, the one that is NOT considered resilient flooring is

   A. linoleum
   B. asphalt tile
   C. vinyl asbestos tile
   D. quarry tile

8. The specifications state: *All exposed surfaces shall be free from knot spots, spalls, ohips, and mineral stains.* The material referred to is MOST likely 8.____

   A. brick B. wood C. marble D. quarry tile

9. A protective transparent coating is to be placed on the aluminum surface of an aluminum window. 9.____
The coating would MOST likely be a transparent coating of

A. gum arable
B. shellac
C. stain
D. lacquer

10. The vertical side of a window frame is known as the 10.____

A. sill B. muntin C. rail D. jamb

11. The specifications state: *Sill and head shall be No. 12 B & S gauge minimum.* 11.____
B & S is an abbreviation of

A. Black & Stone
B. Birmingham & Stone
C. Black & Sloane
D. Brown & Sharpe

12. In three coat plaster, the finish coat follows the brown coat. 12.____
The minimum number of days that must elapse after the brown coat is completed before the finish coat may be applied is MOST NEARLY

A. 1 B. 3 C. 17 D. 32

13. Of the following, the method of construction that is encountering difficulty with governmental agencies because of environmental pollution is 13.____

A. guniting
B. spray painting
C. sprayed on insulation
D. air entraining of concrete

14. The specifications on piping require the use of graphite on cleanout plugs. 14.____
Of the following, the BEST reason for the use of graphite is to

A. facilitate installing the plug
B. facilitate removing the plug
C. make the plug watertight
D. give the plug a dark color for identification purposes

15. The specifications state that the concrete shall have a certain minimum *cement factor.* 15.____
Cement factor is the

A. number of bags of cement per cubic yard of concrete
B. gallons of water per bag of cement
C. number of bags of cement per gallon of water
D. slump of the concrete

16. The specifications state that the ends of a wood beam shall be firecut. 16.____
The end of the beam would appear in place as shown in

A. 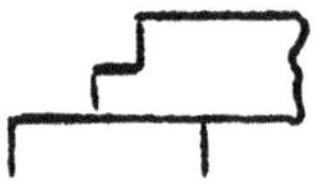 B.  C.  D.

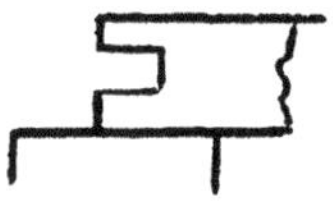

17. One of the unit price items in the contract for extra or omitted work in a building is reinforcing steel in place. 17.____
This price is MOST likely ______ /pound.

A. 12¢ B. 22¢ C. 32¢ D. 42¢

18. The specifications require that porous fill be placed under a concrete slab. 18.____
The material LEAST likely to be permitted as porous fill is

A. crushed stone
B. sand
C. gravel
D. loam

19. Of the following, the organization NOT concerned with standards for construction material is 19.____

A. A.I.S.C. B. A.C.I. C. A.S.T.M. D. A.I.E.M.

20. The specification on grouting states: *The contractor shall furnish all material and labor for properly bedding on Portland cement grout, the equipment or its supporting base.* 20.____
Grout of this type would usually consist of

A. Portland cement only
B. 1 part Portland cement and 1 part sand
C. 1 part Portland cement and 4 parts sand
D. 1 part Portland cement and 8 parts sand

21. Referring to the above question, the thickness of grout for the bases of machinery and equipment normally found in buildings would be, in inches, MOST NEARLY ______ inch(es). 21.____

A. 1/4 B. 1/2 C. 1 D. 3

22. One of the duties of a superintendent is to keep a record of all delays caused by strikes, walkouts, rain, or other causes beyond the contractor's control. 22.____
Of the following, the BEST reason for keeping this record is to

A. penalize the contractor for delays
B. enable the city to plan future jobs more accurately
C. allow the contractor additional time to complete the contract when necessary
D. require the contractor to put on additional forces to meet the contract deadline

23. In setting, the reinforcing steel for a concrete slab 3/8" temperature reinforcing rod interfered with a one inch vertical sleeve for a cold water line. The contractor moved the temperature bar 1/2 inch at the sleeve to avoid the interference. 23.____
This action on the part of the contractor was

A. *improper,* since the bar should have been cut at the point of interference
B. *improper,* since the layout of all the 3/8 inch bars was incorrect according to the plans
C. *proper,* because very minor changes in location of temperature reinforcing steel is permissible
D. *proper,* because cutting steel and placing additional reinforcing steel around the opening would weaken the slab

24. Of the following permits for a new school building, the one NOT issued by the department of buildings is the pernit to 24.____

    A. build
    B. install elevators
    C. erect sidewalk shed when necessary
    D. store material on sidewalk

25. A reinforced concrete canopy is to be constructed. The reinforcing steel would MOST likely appear as in 25.____

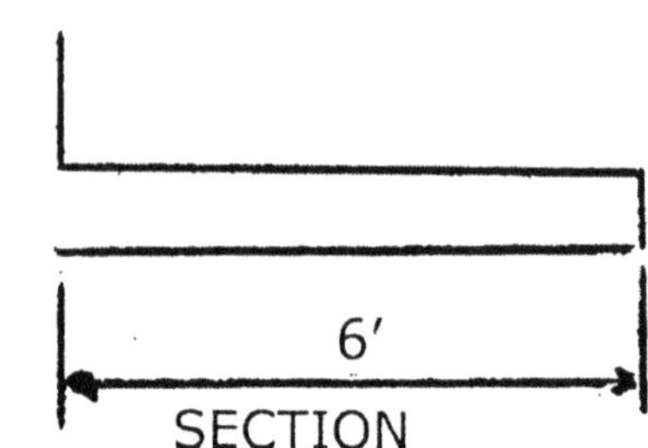

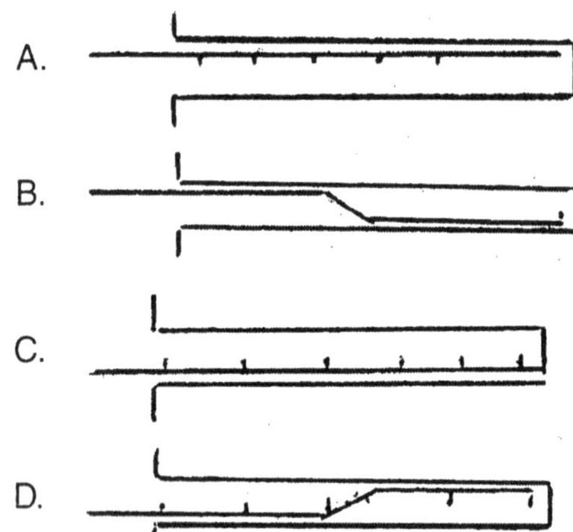

KEY (CORRECT ANSWERS)

1. B
2. B
3. D
4. C
5. D

6. B
7. D
8. C
9. D
10. D

11. D
12. B
13. C
14. B
15. A

16. C
17. B
18. D
19. D
20. B

21. C
22. C
23. C
24. D
25. A

EXAMINATION SECTION
TEST 1

DIRECTIONS: Each question or incomplete statement is followed by several suggested answers or completions. Select the one that BEST answers the question or completes the statement. *PRINT THE LETTER OF THE CORRECT ANSWER IN THE SPACE AT THE RIGHT.*

1. A percentage of the payment for a contract is held back until the job is completed for one year. 1.____
   The MAIN reason for this practice is to insure that the

   A. city doesn't overpay the contractor for the job
   B. contractor will return to correct defective work after the job is completed
   C. contractor will not make unwarranted claims against the city
   D. contractor will pay all his subcontractors

2. There are four separate major contracts on a certain building construction project. 2.____
   The MAJOR disadvantage of this practice, as compared to the practice of having a single contract, is

   A. the difficulty in coordinating the work
   B. the low level of productivity of the tradesman
   C. cost of the material going into the building is greater
   D. the difficulty in finding competent bidders on the contracts

3. Of the following, the PREFERRED way to authorize a contractor to perform work other than required by the contract is by a 3.____

   A. T & M order
   B. unit price order
   C. lump sum modification
   D. change order

4. A contract requires that the prime contractor do a certain minimum percentage of the work with his own forces. 4.____
   Of the following, the BEST reason for this requirement is to

   A. insure good work
   B. discourage bidders who may not have the ability to do the job
   C. encourage more people to bid the job, thus lowering the bid price
   D. freeze out incompetent subcontractors

5. In computing an extra based on the actual cost of work done, the THREE MAJOR items that go into the cost are 5.____

   A. taxes, labor, and material
   B. time, taxes, and material
   C. labor, material, and equipment
   D. taxes, labor, and equipment

6. A contractor is to be penalized if he exceeds a certain completion date. There is a major strike lasting a month that shuts down all construction. 6.____
   Under these conditions, the completion date should be

A. held unchanged
B. made two weeks later than the original date
C. made one month later than the original date
D. made six weeks later than the original completion date

7. The one of the following that refers to a Federal safety program in construction is 7.____

A. OSHA B. AISC C. AIEE D. UL

8. With regard to the placing of concrete, the contractor is GENERALLY 8.____

A. limited to a specific method by the contract
B. not permitted to rent equipment to place the concrete
C. not permitted to pump the concrete into place
D. permitted to choose his own method of placing the concrete

9. The MOST practical control the inspector or resident engineer has over the contractor when the inspector is not satisfied with the quality of the work is to 9.____

A. discuss withholding payment on that part of the work that is unsatisfactory
B. threaten to have the contractor thrown off the job
C. request that the contractor fire the men responsible for the unsatisfactory work
D. call the owner of the company and explain the situation to him

10. The MOST practical method of being sure that the architect will be satisfied with the appearance of the exterior brick work for a building is to 10.____

A. build a sample wall section, for the architect's approval, with the brick that is delivered to the job site
B. send the architect to the plant supplying the brick to insure that the color and tone of the brick is satisfactory
C. have the architect's representative on the job while the brick work is being erected to be sure the finished product is satisfactory
D. put a damage clause in the contract penalizing the contractor if the brick work is not satisfactory to the architect

11. Of the following, the MOST frequent problem that will arise during the construction of a building is 11.____

A. inability to fit all the reinforcing steel in the space allotted to it
B. interference in piping and ductwork
C. inability to keep walls level
D. settling of the foundation as the load comes on the building

12. To find the number of reinforcing bars that should be in a slab, the inspector SHOULD refer to the 12.____

A. architect's plan
B. reinforcing steel design drawings
C. standard detail drawings
D. reinforcing steel detail drawings

13. The specifications for a building state that a certain brick type shall be *Stark Brick type XX or equal.* 13.____
The BEST reason for inserting the *or equal* clause is to

A. permit other companies to compete in supplying the brick
B. allow other companies to submit their product to determine which is best
C. limit the suppliers only to those companies whose product is superior to that produced by Stark
D. allow Stark Brick Company to set the standard for the industry

14. In the absence of a formal training program for inspectors, the BEST of the following ways to train a new man who is to do inspection work is to 14.____

A. give him the literature on the subject so that he can learn what he has to know
B. have him accompany an inspector as the inspector does his work so that he can learn by observing
C. assign him the job and let him learn on his own
D. tell him to go to a school at night that specializes in this field so that he will gain the necessary background

15. Of the following, the safety practice that is REQUIRED on the construction job site is 15.____

A. safety shoes must be worn by all workers
B. safety goggles must be worn by all workers
C. safety helmets must be worn by all workers
D. all workers must have a safety kit in their possession

16. Safety on the job is the concern of 16.____

A. the individual workman only
B. the contractor only
C. all parties on the job
D. the insuring company only

17. Frequently, payments due the contractor are delayed many months because of a backlog of work in the agency. 17.____
This practice is considered

A. *good* because the city saves money by delaying payment
B. *poor* because the contractors will raise their bids in the future to compensate for the added cost
C. *poor* because it becomes difficult to compute payments
D. *good* because it forces the contractor to do good work in order to be sure that he will receive payment

18. Provisions are made in a contract for payment for certain items when delivered to the job before installation. 18.____
The MAIN reason for this practice is to

A. enable better inspection of the items
B. prevent bottlenecks during construction
C. give the contractor a quick profit on the items
D. allow the contractor more time to shop for the items

19. The agency that approves payments to building contractors is the 19.____

A. Corporation Counsel
B. Comptroller's Office
C. Board of Estimate
D. City Planning Commission

20. The bond that the contractor puts up to insure that he will start work is the 20.____

A. Bid Bond
B. Payment Bond
C. Performance Bond
D. Liability Insurance

21. Of the following, the BEST practice to follow in order to minimize claims of damage to adjacent buildings during the construction of a building is to 21.____

A. take out special insurance against such claims
B. make a detailed survey of the condition of the nearby buildings before construction begins
C. make a payment to adjacent property owners in advance so that they waive claims of damage to their property
D. have the buildings underpinned

22. The four MAJOR contracts on a building project are: 22.____

A. General Construction, Electrical, Plumbing and Drainage, Heating, Ventilating and Air Conditioning
B. Plumbing, Heating and Ventilating, Air Conditioning, and General Construction
C. Foundations, Superstructure, Mechanical, and Electrical
D. Air Conditioning, Electrical, Mechanical, and Structural

23. Oil tanks, when set in place inside a building, are frequently filled with water. 23.____
The BEST reason for this practice is

A. to prevent them from floating off their foundation if water fills the room
B. to enable them to be lifted up more easily
C. to prevent them from becoming rusted
D. for emergency use in case of fire

24. The filing system used in the field for correspondence is required to be uniform for all jobs. 24.____
The BEST reason for this requirement is that

A. there is only one good way of setting up the filing system
B. the standardized system is compact, thereby saving space
C. other interested parties such as engineers from the main office will be able to use the files
D. the contractor's forces will understand the filing system and will be able to extract necessary correspondence

25. Upon excavation to the subgrade of a footing to be placed on piles, the inspector finds that the soil is very poor. 25.____
Of the following, the PROPER action for the inspector to take is to

A. do nothing
B. add 20% to the number of piles
C. notify the engineer's office of this condition
D. order the contractor to keep excavating until he hits better soil

26. The general contractor is required to submit a progress schedule before starting work. Of the following, the BEST reason for this requirement is to 26.____

A. determine if the contractor intends to complete the job
B. enable the inspector to determine whether the contractor is on schedule
C. enable the inspector to estimate monthly payments
D. check minority hiring

27. If a contractor is falling behind schedule, the FIRST thing to check if the inspector is looking for the cause of this condition is the 27.____

A. number of men he has on the job
B. efficiency of his crew
C. availability of equipment needed to do the job
D. availability of the latest drawings needed by the contractor

28. The critical path method is a method for 28.____

A. finding the best material needed for a specific use
B. determining the best arrangement of equipment
C. determining the best time to replace a piece of machinery
D. scheduling work

29. The contractor states to the inspector that a given structural detail is undersized and unsafe.
Of the following, the BEST action for the inspector to take in this situation is to 29.____

A. ignore the complaint since the contractor is not an engineer
B. change the detail by issuing a change order
C. notify your superiors of the contractor's statements
D. allow the contractor to modify the detail since it is his responsibility

30. The contractor proposes to use an additive to the concrete to accelerate its set. He asks you, the inspector, for permission to use it.
Of the following, the FIRST action to take in response to his request is to 30.____

A. check if the use of the additive is permitted by the specifications
B. tell him to put the request in writing
C. ask your superior if the use of the additive is acceptable
D. deny him permission since additives to concrete are not permitted

---

KEY (CORRECT ANSWERS)

1.	B	16.	C
2.	A	17.	B
3.	D	18.	B
4.	B	19.	B
5.	C	20.	A
6.	C	21.	B
7.	A	22.	A
8.	D	23.	A
9.	A	24.	C
10.	A	25.	A
11.	B	26.	B
12.	D	27.	A
13.	A	28.	D
14.	B	29.	C
15.	C	30.	A

EXAMINATION SECTION
TEST 1

DIRECTIONS: Each question or incomplete statement is followed by several suggested answers or completions. Select the one that BEST answers the question or completes the statement. *PRINT THE LETTER OF THE CORRECT ANSWER IN THE SPACE AT THE RIGHT.*

1. Of the following, the BEST reason for using vibrators in concrete construction is to 1.____

   A. remove excess water
   B. consolidate the concrete
   C. increase the slump of the concrete
   D. retard the setting of the concrete

2. When a contractor fails to adhere to an approved progress schedule, he should 2.____

   A. revise the schedule without delay
   B. ask for an extension of time on account of delays
   C. adopt such additional means and methods of construction as will make up for the time lost
   D. take no immediate action with the hope that sufficient time will be available later on that will assure the completion in accordance with the schedule

3. The usual contract for work includes a section entitled *Instructions to Bidders* which states that the 3.____

   A. contractor agrees that he has made his own examination and will make no claim for damages on account of errors or omissions
   B. contractor shall not make claims for damages of any discrepancy, error, or omission in any plans
   C. estimates of quantities and calculations are guaranteed by the board to be correct and are deemed to be a representation of the conditions affecting the work
   D. plans, measurements, dimensions, and conditions under which the work is to be performed are guaranteed by the board

4. Specifications covering brickwork usually require special precautions and protection for work in cold weather. 4.____
   The HIGHEST temperature below which these measures are required is *most nearly*

   A. 50° F B. 40° F C. 30° F D. 20° F

5. Controlled concrete is required for the reinforced concrete frame of a large school building. The ultimate strength of this concrete will be *most nearly* ______ pounds per square inch. 5.____

   A. 1000 B. 3000 C. 5000 D. 7000

6. A lump sum type of contract may require the contractor to submit a schedule of unit prices. 6.____
   The BEST reason for this is that it

   A. prevents the lump sum from being too high
   B. simplifies the selection of the lowest bidder

C. enables the estimators to check the total cost
D. provides a means of making equitable partial payments

7. The concrete test that will BEST determine the consistency of a concrete mix is the 7.____

A. slump test
B. sieve analysis
C. calorimetric test
D. water-cement ratio test

8. The BEST way to evaluate the overall state of completion of a construction project is to check the progress estimate against the 8.____

A. inspection work sheet
B. construction schedule
C. inspector's checklist
D. equipment maintenance schedule

Questions 9-15.

DIRECTIONS: Questions 9 through 15 refer to the sketch below.

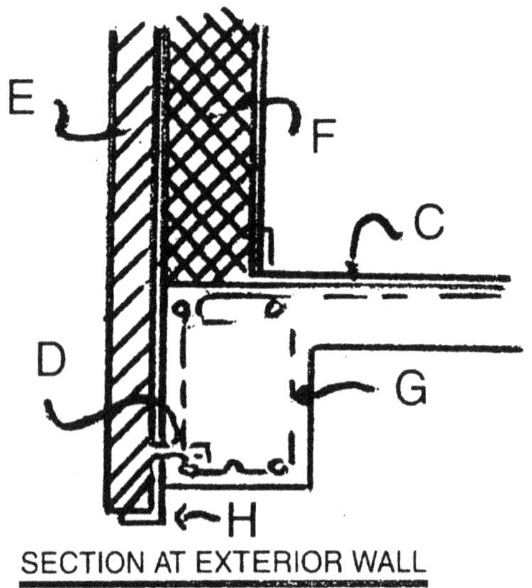

SECTION AT EXTERIOR WALL

9. The floor is made of 9.____

A. air-entrained concrete
B. reinforced concrete
C. lightweight concrete
D. concrete-encased structural steel

10. The exterior wall is a _______ wall. 10.____

A. concrete block
B. cavity construction
C. veneer
D. solid brick

11. Member C is a 11.____

A. deformed bar
B. hooked bar
C. plain bar
D. shear connector

12. Member E is made of 12.____

A. steel B. wood C. brick D. concrete

13. Member F is 13.____

A. concrete block
B. facing brick
C. glazed tile
D. sheetrock

14. Member G is a 14.____

A. longitudinal bar
B. splice
C. stirrup
D. tie wire

15. Member H is a 15.____

A. purlin B. brace C. guy D. lintel

16. A projected sash is a(n) 16.____

A. architectural projection from a building exterior which breaks up a smooth pattern of the wall
B. double-hung window
C. window that opens inward or outward
D. window that has a screen attachment

17. In the construction of cellar concrete floors resting on earth, the item that should be checked MOST carefully is that 17.____

A. the earth is wet before pouring
B. all backfill is granular soil
C. the earth is dry before pouring
D. all backfill is properly compacted

18. Specifications state that column dowels are embedded 24 diameters in the footing. The length of embedment for a number 6 bar is _______ inches. 18.____

A. 6 B. 12 C. 18 D. 24

19. After excavating to the subgrade of a footing, an examination of the soil reveals that it is of a poorer quality than the soil in that area and at that elevation shown on the soil borings. 19.____
Of the following types of footings, the one that would be LEAST affected by this condition is a

A. footing on piles
B. plain concrete footing
C. combined footing
D. spread footing

20. The MAIN reason for requiring written job reports is to 20.____

A. avoid the necessity of oral orders
B. develop better methods of doing the work
C. provide a permanent record of what was done
D. increase the amount of work that can be done

21. Of the following items, the one which should NOT be included in a proposed work schedule is 21.____

    A. a schedule of hourly wage rates and supplementary benefits
    B. an estimated time required for delivery of materials and equipment
    C. the anticipated commencement and completion of the various operations
    D. the sequence and inter-relationship of various operations with those of related contracts

22. A specification requires that brick be laid with *shoved* joints. The BEST reason for this requirement is that it helps the bricklayer to obtain ______ joint(s). 22.____

    A. full
    B. plumb vertical
    C. level horizontal
    D. the required thickness of

23. A specification states that access panels to suspended ceilings will be of metal. The MAIN reason for providing access panels is to 23.____

    A. improve the insulation of the ceiling
    B. improve the appearance of the ceiling
    C. make it easier to construct the building
    D. make it easier to maintain the building

24. A three-coat plaster job is to be 7/8 inches thick. Of the following, the thickness of the individual coats, in inches, would be *most nearly* scratch 24.____

    A. 1/8, brown 1/2, finish 1/4
    B. 3/8, brown 3/8, finish 1/8
    C. 11/16, brown 1/8, finish 1/16
    D. 5/16, brown 1/4, finish 5/16

25. You are assigned to keep a record of the number and volume of all boulders excavated that exceed one cubic yard in volume. The MOST probable reason for this order is: 25.____

    A. Any delays in excavating due to the boulders may result in a claim
    B. The contractor may receive additional payment for rock excavation
    C. There may be an extra charge for hauling boulders from the jobsite
    D. Excavation where there are large boulders involved is dangerous, and in the event of an accident, you will have appropriate records

---

KEY (CORRECT ANSWERS)

1. B
2. C
3. A
4. B
5. B
6. D
7. A
8. B
9. B
10. C
11. B
12. C
13. A
14. C
15. D
16. C
17. D
18. C
19. A
20. C
21. A
22. A
23. D
24. B
25. C

TEST 2

DIRECTIONS: Each question or incomplete statement is followed by several suggested answers or completions. Select the one that BEST answers the question or completes the statement. *PRINT THE LETTER OF THE CORRECT ANSWER IN THE SPACE AT THE RIGHT.*

1. Which one of the following is the PRIMARY object in drawing up a set of specifications for materials to be purchased? 1.___

   A. Control of quality
   B. Outline of intended use
   C. Establishment of standard sizes
   D. Location and method of inspection

2. In order to avoid disputes over payments for extra work in a contract for construction, the BEST procedure to follow would be to 2.___

   A. have contractor submit work progress reports daily
   B. insert a special clause in the contract specifications
   C. have a representative on the job at all times to verify conditions
   D. allocate a certain percentage of the cost of the job to cover such expenses

3. If there is a small amount of water on the surface of a newly-laid concrete sidewalk, the recommended procedure *before* finishing is to 3.___

   A. allow it to evaporate
   B. remove it with a broom
   C. sprinkle some dry cement on top
   D. remove it with a float

4. Prior to the installation of equipment called for in the specifications, the contractor is *usually* required to submit for approval 4.___

   A. sets of shop drawings
   B. a set of revised specifications
   C. a detailed description of the methods of work to be used
   D. a complete list of skilled and unskilled tradesmen he proposes to use

5. A specification on piles states that plumbness must be within 2% of the pile length. If the pile length is 30 feet, the MAXIMUM amount that the pile may be out of plumb is, in inches, *most nearly* 5.___

   A. 5 B. 6 C. 7 D. 8

6. The number of days that it will take high early strength concrete to equal the 28-day strength of normal portland cement concrete is *most nearly* 6.___

   A. 1 B. 3 C. 7 D. 12

7. Specifications may state that a standpipe system will be provided in each building. The MAIN purpose of a standpipe system is to 7.___

   A. supply the roof water tank
   B. provide water for firefighting

C. circulate water for the heating system
D. provide adequate pressure for the water supply

8. The drawing which should be used as a legal reference when checking completed construction work is the _______ drawing. 8.____

A. contract
B. assembly
C. working or shop
D. preliminary

9. Efflorescence may BEST be removed from brickwork by washing with a solution of _______ acid. 9.____

A. muriatic
B. citric
C. carbonic
D. nitric

10. The MAIN difference between sheet glass and plate glass is 10.____

A. the surface finish of the two types of glass
B. the heat absorbing qualities of the two types of glass
C. plate glass is thinner than sheet glass
D. plate glass is tempered while sheet glass is not tempered

11. Construction joints in the concrete columns of a multistory building are *usually* located 11.____

A. at floor level
B. 1 foot above floor level
C. at the underside of floor slab
D. at the underside of deepest beam framing into the column

12. A contractor on a large construction project *usually* receives partial payments based on 12.____

A. estimates of completed work
B. actual cost of materials delivered and work completed
C. estimates of material delivered and not paid for by the contractor
D. the breakdown estimate submitted after the contract was signed and prorated over the estimated duration of the contract

13. According to the building code, masonry footings shall extend at least 4' below finished grade. 13.____
The PRIMARY reason for this is to

A. get below the frost line
B. make the foundation stronger
C. keep water out of the basement
D. reach a lower soil strata where better bearing material can be found

14. Good inspection methods require that the inspector 14.____

A. be observant and check all details
B. constantly check with the engineer who designed the school
C. apply specifications according to his interpretation
D. permit slight job variation to establish good public relations

Questions 15-19.

DIRECTIONS: Questions 15 through 19 refer to the following specification for wood flooring. In answering these questions, refer to this specification.

2" x 4" wood sleepers laid flat @ 16" o.c.
1" x 6" sub flooring, laid diagonally; cut at butt joints with parallel cuts; joints at center of sleepers, well staggered, no two joints side by side. Not less than 1/8" space between boards.
One layer of 15# asphalt felt on top of sub-floor.
Finish floor - North Rock Maple, T & G, laid perpendicular to sleepers; 8d nails not more than 12" apart; end joints well scattered with at least 2 flooring strips between joints.
Flooring 25/32" x 2 1/4" face - 1st quality.

15. It is *most likely* that the floor referred to in the specification is to be laid 15.___

A. directly on the ground
B. on a concrete base
C. on wood joists
D. on steel beams

16. The BEST reason for specifying that the sub-flooring be parallel cut at butt joints is that this 16.___

A. requires less material
B. provides staggered joints
C. provides more nailing surface
D. allows the joint to fall between sleepers

17. The BEST reason for specifying a minimum space between the sub-floor boards is that it 17.___

A. saves on material
B. reduces creaking
C. allows for expansion
D. prevents dry rot

18. The BEST reason for specifying at least 2 flooring strips between joints in the finish flooring is that 18.___

A. it looks better
B. it is more economical
C. each board is supported by two adjoining boards
D. each finish board is supported by at least two sub-floor boards

19. The BEST reason for placing asphalt felt on top of the sub-floor is to 19.___

A. deaden noise
B. preserve the wood
C. reduce dampness
D. permit movement

20. Assume you are recommending in a report to your superior that a radical change in a standard maintenance procedure should be adopted. 20.___
Of the following, the MOST important information to be included in this report is

A. a list of the reasons for making this change
B. the names of the other GSSM who favor the change
C. a complete description of the present procedure
D. amount of training time needed for the new procedure

21. Specifications require that the first floor beams of a building must be in place before backfill is placed against the foundation walls. 21.____
The BEST reason for this requirement is that

A. without the first floor beams in place, the wall may become overstressed
B. it is easier to inspect the first floor construction when the backfill is not in place
C. the utilities up to the first floor level should be in place before backfill is placed
D. the boiler setting hung from the first floor must be in place before backfill is placed

22. The frequency with which job reports are submitted should depend MAINLY on 22.____

A. how comprehensive the report has to be
B. the amount of information in the report
C. the availability of an experienced man to write the report
D. the importance of changes in the information included in the report

23. Assume that a contractor proposed to start the roofing three days after pouring the concrete roof slab. 23.____
This proposal is

A. *good,* mainly since it will speed the construction
B. *good,* mainly since it will assist in curing the concrete
C. *poor* in cold weather but is all right in warm weather
D. *poor,* mainly since excess water in the concrete may bulge the roofing

24. In performing field inspectional work, an inspector is the contact man between the public and the board, and it is his job to secure compliance through the maximum utilization of persuasion and education and the minimum application of coercion. 24.____
According to the above statement, an inspector performing inspectional duties should

A. seek to obtain voluntary compliance and use coercion only as a last resort
B. be conciliatory on all issues of non-compliance and not take an attitude of firmness and authority
C. maintain a strictly impersonal attitude in the exercise of his duties at all times
D. use the threat of legal action to secure conformance with specified requirements

25. A specification requires that brick should be thoroughly wet before using. 25.____
Of the following, the BEST reason for this requirement is that

A. wetting the brick uncovers hidden flaws
B. it is easier to shove wet brick into place
C. wetting cleans the pores of the brick ensuring a stronger bond
D. wetting decreases absorption of water from the mortar

KEY (CORRECT ANSWERS)

1. A
2. C
3. A
4. A
5. C
6. C
7. B
8. A
9. A
10. A
11. A
12. A
13. A
14. A
15. B
16. C
17. C
18. C
19. C
20. A
21. A
22. D
23. D
24. A
25. D

TEST 3

DIRECTIONS: Each question or incomplete statement is followed by several suggested answers or completions. Select the one that BEST answers the question or completes the statement. *PRINT THE LETTER OF THE CORRECT ANSWER IN THE SPACE AT THE RIGHT.*

Questions 1-4.

DIRECTIONS: Questions 1 to 4 refer to the sketch below.

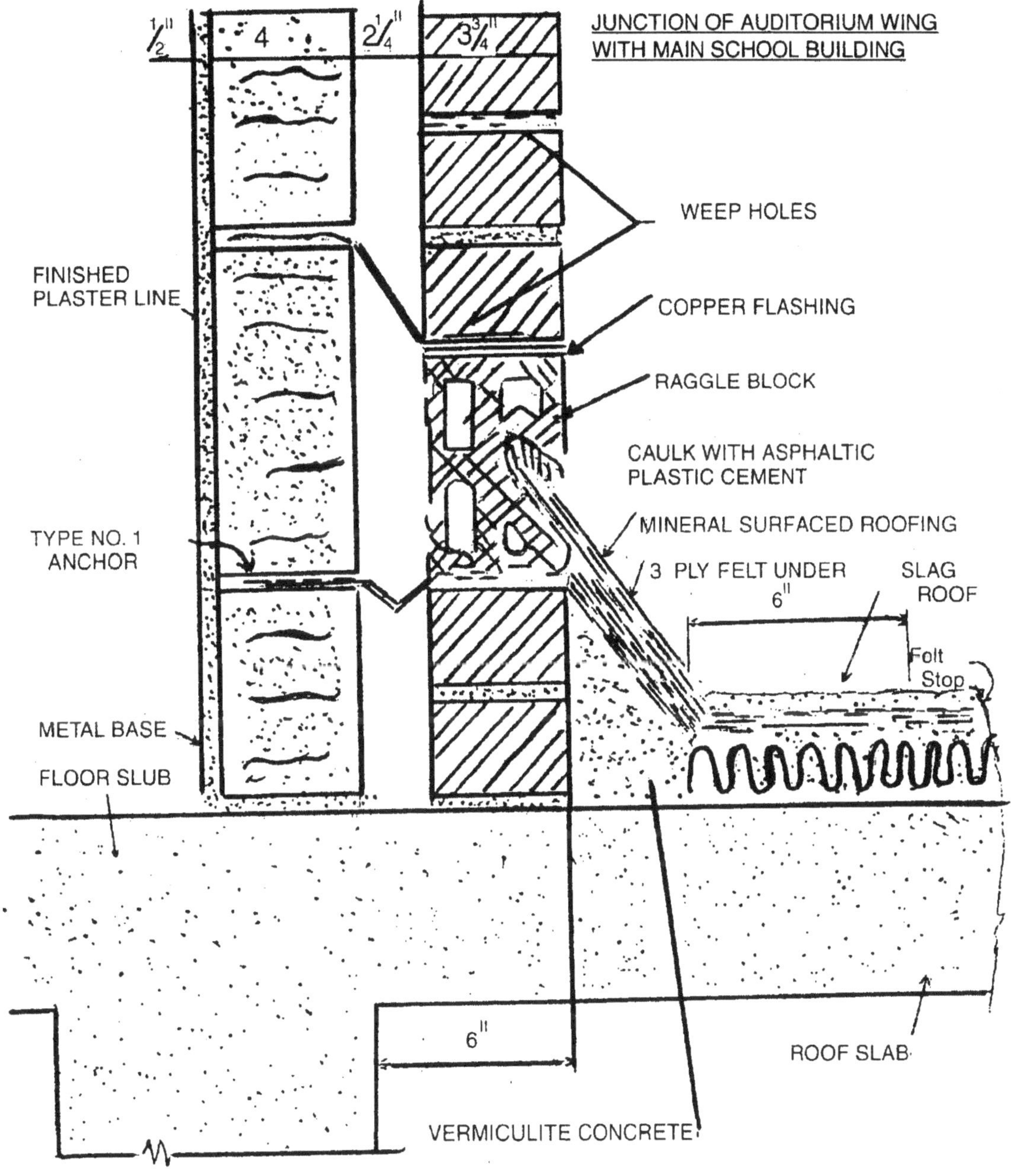

1. The 1/2" of plaster would *most likely* be applied in ______ coats. 1.____

A. one B. two C. three D. four

2. Vermiculite concrete is PRIMARILY _______ concrete. 2._____

A. low-slump
B. water-resistant
C. an air-entrained
D. a lightweight

3. Which of the following statements relating to copper flashing is CORRECT? It 3._____

A. is perforated in the air space
B. consists of one solid continuous sheet
C. consists of 2-inch strips spaced every foot
D. is provided to prevent the fall of mortar into the air space

4. The 4-inch thick material is *most likely* 4._____

A. cinder block
B. gypsum block
C. brick
D. terra cotta

5. A rowlock course of brick is one in which the bricks are laid 5._____

A. on their 2 1/4" x 8" surface
B. in an interlocking fashion
C. with dowels at set intervals
D. in a one-header followed by a one-stretcher course

6. Specifications for excavation for spread footings require that machine excavation be to within a foot of the final subgrade and the remainder of the excavation shall be by hand. The BEST reason for this requirement is to 6._____

A. prevent cave-ins near the excavation
B. cut down on the amount of fill needed
C. prevent excavation below the subgrade
D. insure that the area in the vicinity of the footing not be excessively disturbed

7. The CHIEF purpose in preparing an outline for a report is *usually* to insure that 7._____

A. the report will be grammatically correct
B. every point will be given equal emphasis
C. principal and secondary points will be properly integrated
D. the language of the report will be of the same level and include the same technical terms

8. One of the properties of tempered plate glass which affects installation is that it 8._____

A. has a blue tinge
B. cannot be cut after the glass is tempered
C. does not bond with putty or glazing compound
D. cracks more easily than ordinary plate glass

9. In assigning the men to various jobs, the BEST principle for a supervisor to follow is to 9._____

A. study the men's abilities and assign them accordingly
B. rotate a man from job to job until you find one which he can do well
C. assign each of them to a job and let them adjust to it in their own way
D. assume that men appointed to the position can do all parts of the work equally well

10. With respect to waterproofing existing basements, the MOST effective and lasting repairs are those made 10.____

    A. on the earth side of a basement wall
    B. on the inside basement wall surface
    C. on the floor
    D. in the mortar joints

11. During the actual construction work, the CHIEF value of a construction schedule is to 11.____

    A. insure that the work will be done on time
    B. reveal when production is behind schedule
    C. show how much equipment and material is required for the project
    D. furnish data as to the methods and techniques of construction operations

12. When building the formwork for a 12" doubly reinforced concrete wall, the USUAL order of construction is place the 12.____

    A. formwork for both faces of the wall; then place the reinforcing steel
    B. reinforcing steel and then place the formwork for both faces of the wall
    C. formwork for one face of the wall, place the reinforcing steel, and then place the formwork for the other face of the wall
    D. formwork for one face of the wall, place the reinforcing steel for one face, place the formwork for the other face of the wall, and then place the reinforcement for the second face

13. The GREATEST period of time must elapse between 13.____

    A. pouring and stripping concrete formwork
    B. placing reinforcing steel and pouring concrete
    C. applying the finish plaster coat and painting a plastered wall
    D. applying the first and second coats of a 3-coat plaster job for a wall

14. A fixed amount of money is generally withheld from the contractor for a definite period after the completion of construction.
    The BEST reason for this is 14.____

    A. that the money will be available for taxes due
    B. to penalize the contractor for poor work
    C. that it is a security for the repair of any defective work
    D. that the money will be available for modifications in the design of the structure

15. The practice of applying the brown coat to a wall on the day after the scratch coat of gypsum plaster was applied is GENERALLY considered 15.____

    A. satisfactory
    B. satisfactory only if the temperature is between 50° and 70° F
    C. unsatisfactory because 7 days must elapse between the application of the scratch and brown coats
    D. unsatisfactory because at least 3 days must elapse between the application of the scratch and brown coats

16. Fiberboard material 2 inches thick is placed on a flat reinforced concrete roof. The PRIMARY function of this 2 inch thick material is to 16.____

A. act as a vapor barrier
B. soundproof the rooms below
C. prevent loss of heat from the building
D. keep water from penetrating the ceiling below

17. The PRIMARY purpose of adding lime to a mortar mix is to 17.____

A. improve the appearance of the mortar
B. increase the workability of the mortar
C. increase the strength of the mortar
D. improve the bearing capacity of the wall

18. Assume that excavation is taking place adjacent to a building on a spread footing and a building on pile foundations. 18.____
Extreme care must be exercised in excavating

A. near the pile-supported building because the soil in the area is of poor quality
B. near a building on spread footings because the concrete footings may crack
C. for a pile-supported foundation because heavy loads are involved
D. near a building on spread footings because of the danger of undermining the foundations

19. An inspector inspecting a large building under construction inspected brickwork at 9 M., formwork at 10 A.M., and concrete at 11 A.M. and did his office work in the afternoon. He followed the same pattern daily for months. 19.____
This procedure is

A. *bad* because not enough time is devoted to concrete work
B. *bad* because the tradesmen know when the inspections will occur
C. *good* because it is methodical and he does not miss any of the trades
D. *good* because it gives equal amount of time to the important trades

20. If a supervisor finds a discrepancy between the plans and specifications, he should 20.____

A. always follow the plans
B. ask for an interpretation
C. always follow the specifications
D. follow the plans if the difference is in dimensions

KEY (CORRECT ANSWERS)

1. B
2. D
3. B
4. A
5. A

6. D
7. C
8. B
9. A
10. A

11. B
12. C
13. C
14. C
15. A

16. C
17. B
18. D
19. B
20. B

READING COMPREHENSION
UNDERSTANDING AND INTERPRETING WRITTEN MATERIAL
EXAMINATION SECTION
TEST 1

DIRECTIONS: Each question or incomplete statement is followed by-several suggested answers or completions. Select the one that BEST answers the question or completes the statement. *PRINT THE LETTER OF THE CORRECT ANSWER IN THE SPACE AT THE RIGHT.*

Questions 1-3.

DIRECTIONS: Questions 1 through 3, inclusive, are to be answered in accordance with the following paragraph.

All cement work contracts, more or less, in setting. The contraction in concrete walls and other structures causes fine cracks to develop at regular intervals. The tendency to contract increases in direct proportion to the quantity of cement in the concrete. A rich mixture will contract more than a lean mixture. A concrete wall which has been made of a very lean mixture and which has been built by filling only about one foot in depth of concrete in the form each day will frequently require close inspection to reveal the cracks.

1. According to the above paragraph, 1.____

    A. shrinkage seldom occurs in concrete
    B. shrinkage occurs only in certain types of concrete
    C. by placing concrete at regular intervals, shrinkage may be avoided
    D. it is impossible to prevent shrinkage

2. According to the above paragraph, the one of the factors which reduces shrinkage in concrete is the 2.____

    A. volume of concrete in wall
    B. height of each day's pour
    C. length of wall
    D. length and height of wall

3. According to the above paragraph, a rich mixture 3.____

    A. pours the easiest
    B. shows the largest amount of cracks
    C. is low in cement content
    D. need not be inspected since cracks are few

Questions 4-6.

DIRECTIONS: Questions 4 through 6, inclusive, are to be answered SOLELY on the basis of the following paragraph.

It is best to avoid surface water on freshly poured concrete in the first place. However, when there is a very small amount present, the recommended procedure is to allow it to evaporate before finishing. If there is considerable water, it is removed with a broom, belt, float, or by other convenient means. It is never good practice to sprinkle dry cement, or a mixture of cement and fine aggregate, on concrete to take up surface water. Such fine materials form a layer on the surface that is likely to dust or hair check when the concrete hardens.

4. The MAIN subject of the above passage is 4.____

   A. surface cracking of concrete
   B. evaporation of water from freshly poured concrete
   C. removing surface water from concrete
   D. final adjustments of ingredients in the concrete mix

5. According to the above passage, the sprinkling of dry cement on the surface of a concrete mix would MOST LIKELY 5.____

   A. prevent the mix from setting
   B. cause discoloration on the surface of the concrete
   C. cause the coarse aggregate to settle out too quickly
   D. cause powdering and small cracks on the surface of the concrete

6. According to the above passage, the thing to do when considerable surface water is present on the freshly poured concrete is to 6.____

   A. dump the concrete back into the mixer and drain the water
   B. allow the water to evaporate before finishing
   C. remove the water with a broom, belt, or float
   D. add more fine aggregate but not cement

Questions 7-9.

DIRECTIONS: Questions 7 through 9, inclusive, are to be answered ONLY in accordance with the information given in the paragraph below.

Before placing the concrete, check that the forms are rigid and well braced and place the concrete within 45 minutes after mixing it. Fill the forms to the top with the wearing-course concrete. Level off the surfaces with a strieboard. When the concrete becomes stiff but still workable (in a few hours), finish the surface with a wood float. This fills the hollows and compacts the concrete and produces a smooth but gritty finish. For a non-gritty and smoother surface (but one that is more slippery when wet), follow up with a steel trowel after the water sheen from the wood-troweling starts to disappear. If you wish, slant the tread forward a fraction of an inch so that it will shed rain water.

7. Slanting the tread a fraction of an inch gives a surface that will 7.____

   A. have added strength
   B. not be slippery when wet
   C. shed rain water
   D. not have hollows

8. In addition to giving a smooth but gritty finish, the use of a wood float will tend to 8.____

   A. give a finish that is slippery when wet
   B. compact the concrete
   C. give a better wearing course
   D. provide hollows to retain rain water

9. Which one of the following statements is most nearly correct? 9.____

   A. Having checked the forms, one may place the concrete immediately after mixing same.
   B. One must wait at least 15 minutes after mixing the concrete before it may be placed in the forms.
   C. A gritty compact finish and one which is more slippery when wet will result with the use of a wood float.
   D. A steel trowel used promptly after a wood float will tend to give a non-gritty smooth finish.

Questions 10-11.

DIRECTIONS: Questions 10 and 11 are to be answered SOLELY on the basis of information contained in the following paragraph.

Tools and plastering methods have changed very little over the years. Most of the changes are mere improvements of the basic tools. The tools formerly made by hand are now machine-made and are *rigidly* constructed of light, but strong, materials in contrast to the clumsy constructions of the early types. The power-driven mixers and hoisting equipment used on large plastering jobs today produce better mortars and lighten the tasks involved.

10. According to the above paragraph, present day tools used for plastering 10.____

    A. have made plastering much more complicated than it used to be
    B. are heavier than the old-fashioned tools they replaced
    C. produce poorer results but speed up the job
    D. are lighter and stronger than the hand-made tools of the past

11. As used in the above paragraph, the word *rigidly* means MOST NEARLY 11.____

    A. feeble B. weakly C. firmly D. flexibly

Questions 12-18.

DIRECTIONS: Questions 12 through 18 are to be answered in accordance with the following paragraphs.

SURFACE RENEWING OVERLAYS

A surface renewing overlay should consist of material which can be constructed in very thin layers. The material must fill surface voids and provide an impervious skid-resistant surface. It must also be sufficiently resistant to traffic abrasion to provide an economical service life.

Materials meeting these requirements are:

a. Asphalt concrete having small particle size
b. Hot sand asphalts
c. Surface seal coats

Fine-graded asphalt concrete or hot sand asphalt can be constructed in layers as thin as one-half inch and fulfill all requirements for surface renewing overlays. They are recommended for thin resurfacing of pavements having high traffic volumes, as their service lives are relatively long when constructed properly. They can be used for minor leveling, they are quiet riding, and their appearance is exceptionally pleasing. Seal coats or slurry seals may fulfill surface requirements for low traffic pavements.

12. A surface renewing overlay must fill surface voids, provide an impervious skid-resistant surface, and 12.____

A. be resistant to traffic abrasion
B. have small particle size
C. be exceptionally pleasing in appearance
D. be constructed in half-inch layers

13. An *impervious skid-resistant surface* means a surface that is 13.____

A. rough to the touch and fixed firmly in place
B. waterproof and provides good gripping for tires
C. not damaged by skidding vehicles
D. smooth to the touch and quiet riding

14. The number of types of materials that can be constructed in very thin layers and are also suitable for surface renewing overlays is 14.____

A. 1 B. 2 C. 3 D. 4

15. The SMALLEST thickness of asphalt concrete or hot sand asphalt that can fulfill all requirements for surface renewing overlays is ______ inch(es). 15.____

A. ¼ B. ½ C. 1 D. 2

16. The materials that are recommended for thin resurfacing of pavements having high traffic volumes are 16.____

A. those that have relatively long service lives
B. asphalt concretes with maximum particle size
C. surface seal coats
D. slurry seals with voids

17. Fine-graded asphalt concrete and hot sand asphalt are quiet riding and are also 17.____

A. recommended for low traffic pavements
B. used as slurry seal coats
C. suitable for major leveling
D. exceptionally pleasing in appearance

18. The materials that may fulfill surface requirements for low traffic pavements are 18.____

A. fine-graded asphalt concretes
B. hot sand asphalts
C. seal coats or slurry seals
D. those that can be used for minor leveling

Questions 19-25.

DIRECTIONS: Questions 19 through 25 are to be answered SOLELY on the basis of the paragraphs below.

OPEN-END WRENCHES

Solid, non-adjustable wrenches with openings in one or both ends are called open-end wrenches. Wrenches with small openings are usually shorter than wrenches with large openings. This proportions the lever advantage of the wrench to the bolt or stud and helps prevent wrench breakage or damage to the bolt or stud.

Open-end wrenches may have their jaws parallel to the handle or at angles anywhere up to 90 degrees. The average angle is 15 degrees. This angular displacement variation permits selection of a wrench suited for places where there is room to make only a part of a complete turn of a nut or bolt. Handles are usually straight, but may be curved. Those with curved handles are called S-wrenches. Other open-end wrenches may have offset handles. This allows the head to reach nut or bolt heads that are sunk below the surface.

There are a few basic rules that you should keep in mind when using wrenches. They are:

I. ALWAYS use a wrench that fits the nut properly. Otherwise, the wrench may slip, or the nut may be damaged.
II. Keep wrenches clean and free from oil. Otherwise, they may slip, resulting in possible serious injury to you or damage to the work.
III. Do NOT increase the leverage of a wrench by placing a pipe over the handle. Increased leverage may damage the wrench or the work.

19. Open-end wrenches 19.____

A. are adjustable
B. are solid
C. always have openings at both ends
D. are always S-shaped

20. Wrench proportions are such that wrenches with ______ openings have ______ handles. 20.____

A. larger; shorter
B. smaller; longer
C. larger; longer
D. smaller; thicker

21. The average angle between the jaws and the handle of a wrench is ______ degrees. 21.____

A. 0
B. 15
C. 22
D. 90

22. Offset handles are intended for use MAINLY with 22.____

A. offset nuts
B. bolts having fine threads
C. nuts sunk below the surface
D. bolts that permit limited swing

23. The wrench which is selected should fit the nut properly because this 23.____

A. prevents distorting the wrench
B. insures use of all wrench sizes
C. avoids damaging the nut
D. overstresses the bolt

24. Oil on wrenches is 24.____

A. *good* because it prevents rust
B. *good* because it permits easier turning
C. *bad* because the wrench may slip off the nut
D. *bad* because the oil may spoil the work

25. Extending the handle of a wrench by slipping a piece of pipe over it is considered 25.____

A. *good* because it insures a tight nut
B. *good* because less effort is needed to loosen a nut
C. *bad* because the wrench may be damaged
D. *bad* because the amount of tightening can not be controlled

---

KEY (CORRECT ANSWERS)

1. D
2. B
3. B
4. C
5. D

6. C
7. C
8. B
9. A
10. D

11. C
12. A
13. B
14. C
15. B

16. A
17. D
18. C
19. B
20. C

21. B
22. C
23. C
24. C
25. C

TEST 2

DIRECTIONS: Each question or incomplete statement is followed by several suggested answers or completions. Select the one that BEST answers the question or completes the statement. *PRINT THE LETTER OF THE CORRECT ANSWER IN THE SPACE AT THE RIGHT.*

Questions 1-3.

DIRECTIONS: Questions 1 through 3 are to be answered SOLELY on the basis of the following passage.

A utility plan is a floor plan which shows the layout of a heating, electrical, plumbing, or other utility system. Utility plans are used primarily by the persons reponsible for the utilities, but they are important to the craftsman as well. Most utility installations require the leaving of openings in walls, floors, and roofs for the admission or installation of utility features. The craftsman who is, for example, pouring a concrete foundation wall must study the utility plans to determine the number, sizes, and locations of the openings he must leave for piping, electric lines, and the like.

1. The one of the following items of information which is LEAST likely to be provided by a utility plan is the 1.____

   A. location of the joists and frame members around stairwells
   B. location of the hot water supply and return piping
   C. location of light fixtures
   D. number of openings in the floor for radiators

2. According to the passage, the persons who will *most likely* have the GREATEST need for the information included in a utility plan of a building are those who 2.____

   A. maintain and repair the heating system
   B. clean the premises
   C. paint housing exteriors
   D. advertise property for sale

3. According to the passage, a repair crew member should find it MOST helpful to consult a utility plan when information is needed about the 3.____

   A. thickness of all doors in the structure
   B. number of electrical outlets located throughout the structure
   C. dimensions of each window in the structure
   D. length of a roof rafter

Questions 4-9.

DIRECTIONS: Questions 4 through 9 are to be answered SOLELY on the basis of the following passage.

The basic hand-operated hoisting device is the tackle or purchase, consisting of a line called a fall, reeved through one or more blocks. To hoist a load of given size, you must set up a rig with a safe working load equal to or in excess of the load to be hoisted. In order to do this, you must be able to calculate the safe working load of a single part of line of given size, the safe working load of a given purchase which contains a line of given size, and the minimum size of hooks or shackles which you must use in a given type of purchase to hoist a given load. You must also be able to calculate the thrust which a given load will exert on a gin pole or a set of shears inclined at a given angle, the safe working load which a spar of a given size used as a gin pole or as one of a set of shears will sustain, and the stress which a given load will set up in the back guy of a gin pole or in the back guy of a set of shears inclined at a given angle.

4. The above passage refers to the lifting of loads by means of 4.____

A. erected scaffolds
B. manual rigging devices
C. power-driven equipment
D. conveyor belts

5. It can be concluded from the above passage that a set of shears serves to 5.____

A. absorb the force and stress of the working load
B. operate the tackle
C. contain the working load
D. compute the safe working load

6. According to the above passage, a spar can be used for a 6.____

A. back guy
B. block
C. fall
D. gin pole

7. According to the above passage, the rule that a user of hand-operated tackle MUST follow is to make sure that the safe working load is AT LEAST 7.____

A. equal to the weight of the given load
B. twice the combined weight of the block and falls
C. one-half the weight of the given load
D. twice the weight of the given load

8. According to the above passage, the two parts that make up a tackle are 8.____

A. back guys and gin poles
B. blocks and falls
C. rigs and shears
D. spars and shackles

9. According to the above passage, in order to determine whether it is safe to hoist a particular load, you MUST 9.____

A. use the maximum size hooks
B. time the speed to bring a given load to a desired place
C. calculate the forces exerted on various types of rigs
D. repeatedly lift and lower various loads

Questions 10-15.

DIRECTIONS: Questions 10 through 15 are to be answered SOLELY on the basis of the following set of instructions.

PATCHING SIMPLE CRACKS IN A BUILT-UP ROOF

If there is a visible crack in built-up roofing, the repair is simple and straightforward:

1. With a brush, clean all loose gravel and dust out of the crack, and clean three or four inches around all sides of it.
2. With a trowel or putty knife, fill the crack with asphalt cement and then spread a layer of asphalt cement about 1/8 inch thick over the cleaned area.
3. Place a strip of roofing felt big enough to cover the crack into the wet cement and press it down firmly.
4. Spread a second layer of cement over the strip of felt and well past its edges.
5. Brush gravel back over the patch.

10. According to the above passage, in order to patch simple cracks in a built-up roof, it is necessary to use a 10.____

A. putty knife and a drill
B. knife and pliers
C. tack hammer and a punch
D. brush and a trowel

11. According to the above passage, the size of the area that should be clear of loose gravel and dust before the asphalt cement is first applied should 11.____

A. be the exact size of the crack itself
B. extend three or four inches on all sides of the crack
C. be 1/8 inch greater than the size of the crack itself
D. extend the length of the roofing strip

12. According to the above passage, loose gravel and dust in the crack should be removed with a 12.____

A. brush
B. felt pad
C. trowel
D. dust mop

13. Assume that both layers of asphalt cement needed to patch the crack are of the same thickness.
The total thickness of asphalt cement used in the patch should be MOST NEARLY ______ inch. 13.____

A. 1/2
B. 1/3
C. 1/4
D. 1/8

14. According to the instructions in the above passage, how large should the strip of roofing felt be cut? 14.____

A. Three of four inches square
B. Smaller than the crack and small enough to be surrounded by cement on all sides of the strip
C. Exactly the same size and shape of the area covered by the wet cement
D. Large enough to completely cover the crack

15. The final or finishing action to be taken in patching a simple crack in a built-up roof is to 15.____

A. clean out the inside of the crack
B. spread a layer of asphalt a second time
C. cover the crack with roofing felt
D. cover the patch of roofing felt and cement with gravel

Questions 16-17.

DIRECTIONS: Questions 16 and 17 are to be answered SOLELY on the basis of the information given in the following paragraph.

Supplies are to be ordered from the stockroom once a week. The standard requisition form, Form SP21, is to be used for ordering all supplies. The form is prepared in triplicate, one white original and two green copies. The white and one green copy are sent to the stockroom, and the remaining green copy is to be kept by the orderer until the supplies are received.

16. According to the above paragraph, there is a limit on the 16.____

A. amount of supplies that may be ordered
B. day on which supplies may be ordered
C. different kinds of supplies that may be ordered
D. number of times supplies may be ordered in one year

17. According to the above paragraph, when the standard requisition form for supplies is prepared, 17.____

A. a total of four requisition blanks is used
B. a white form is the original
C. each copy is printed in two colors
D. one copy is kept by the stock clerk

Questions 18-21.

DIRECTION: Questions 18 through 21 are to be answered SOLELY on the basis of the following passage.

The Oil Pollution Act for U. S. waters defines an *oily mixture* as 100 parts or more of oil in one million parts of mixture. This mixture is not allowed to be discharged into the prohibited zone. The prohibited zone may, in special cases, be extended 100 miles out to sea but, in general, remains at 50 miles offshore. The United States Coast Guard must be contacted to report all *oily mixture* spills. The Federal Water Pollution Control Act provides for a fine of $10,000 for failure to notify the United States Coast Guard. An employer may take action against an employee if the employee causes an *oily mixture* spill. The law holds your employer responsible for either cleaning up or paying for the removal of the oil spillage.

18. According to the Oil Pollution Act, an *oily mixture* is defined as one in which there are ______ parts or more of oil in ______ parts of mixture. 18.____

A. 50; 10,000
B. 100; 10,000
C. 100; 1,000,000
D. 10,000; 1,000,000

19. Failure to notify the proper authorities of an *oily mixture* spill is punishable by a fine. Such fine is provided for by the 19.____

A. United States Coast Guard
B. Federal Water Pollution Control Act
C. Oil Pollution Act
D. United States Department of Environmental Protection

20. According to the law, the one responsible for the removal of an *oily mixture* spilled into U.S. waters is the 20.____

A. employer
B. employee
C. U.S. Coast Guard
D. U.S. Pollution Control Board

21. The *prohibited zone,* in general, is the body of water 21.____

A. within 50 miles offshore
B. beyond 100 miles offshore
C. within 10,000 yards of the coastline
D. beyond 10,000 yards from the coastline

Questions 22-25.

DIRECTIONS: Questions 22 through 25 are to be answered SOLELY on the basis of the following paragraph.

Synthetic detergents are materials produced from petroleum products or from animal or vegetable oils and fats. One of their advantages is the fact that they can be made to meet a particular cleaning problem by altering the foaming, wetting, and emulsifying properties of a cleaner. They are added to commonly used cleaning materials such as solvents, water, and alkalies to improve their cleaning performance. The adequate wetting of the surface to be cleaned is paramount in good cleaning performance. Because of the relatively high surface tension of water, it has poor wetting ability, unless its surface tension is decreased by addition of a detergent or soap. This allows water to flow into crevices and around small particles of soil, thus loosening them.

22. According to the above paragraph, synthetic detergents are made from all of the following EXCEPT 22.____

A. petroleum products
B. vegetable oils
C. surface tension oils
D. animal fats

23. According to the above paragraph, water's poor wetting ability is related to 23.____

A. its low surface tension
B. its high surface tension
C. its vegetable oil content
D. the amount of dirt on the surface to be cleaned

24. According to the above paragraph, synthetic detergents are added to all of the following EXCEPT 24.____

A. alkalines
B. water
C. acids
D. solvents

25. According to the above paragraph, altering a property of a cleaner can give an advantage in meeting a certain cleaning problem. 25.____
The one of the following that is NOT a property altered by synthetic detergents is the cleaner's

A. flow ability
B. foaming property
C. emulsifying property
D. wetting ability

KEY (CORRECT ANSWERS)

1. A
2. A
3. B
4. B
5. A
6. D
7. A
8. B
9. C
10. D
11. B
12. A
13. C
14. D
15. D
16. D
17. B
18. C
19. B
20. A
21. A
22. C
23. B
24. C
25. A

ARITHMETICAL REASONING

EXAMINATION SECTION
TEST 1

DIRECTIONS: Each question or incomplete statement is followed by several suggested answers or completions. Select the one that BEST answers the question or completes the statement. *PRINT THE LETTER OF THE CORRECT ANSWER IN THE SPACE AT THE RIGHT.*

1. If it takes 2 men 9 days to do a job, how many men are needed to do the same job in 3 days? 1.____

   A. 4 B. 5 C. 6 D. 7

2. Suppose that a department operates 1,644 buildings. If one employee is needed for every 2 buildings, and one foreman is needed for every 18 employees, the number of foremen needed is CLOSEST to 2.____

   A. 45 B. 50 C. 55 D. 60

3. If 60 bars of soap cost the same as 2 gallons of wax, how many bars of soap can be bought for the price of 5 gallons of wax? 3.____

   A. 120 B. 150 C. 180 D. 300

4. An employee waxes 275 sq.ft. of floor on Monday, 352 sq.ft. on Tuesday, 179 sq.ft. on Wednesday, and 302 sq.ft. on Thursday. 4.____
   In order to average 280 sq.ft. of floor waxed a day, how many square feet of floor must he wax on Friday?

   A. 264 B. 278 C. 292 D. 358

5. A project covers 35 acres altogether. Lawns, playgrounds, and walks take up 28 acres and the rest is given over to buildings. 5.____
   What percentage of the total area is given over to buildings?

   A. 7% B. 20% C. 25% D. 28%

6. When preparing for a mopping operation, fill the standard 16 quart bucket to the 3/4 full mark with warm water. Then add detergent at the rate of 2 oz. per gallon of water and disinfectant at the rate of 1 oz. to 3 gallons of water. According to these directions, the amount of detergent and disinfectant to add to 3/4 of a bucket of warm water is _____ oz. detergent and _____ oz. disinfectant. 6.____

   A. 4; 1/2 B. 5; 3/4 C. 6; 1 D. 8; 1 1/4

7. If corn brooms weigh 32 lbs. a dozen, the average weight of one corn broom is CLOSEST to _____ lbs. _____ oz. 7.____

   A. 2; 14 B. 2; 11 C. 2; 9 D. 2; 6

8. At the beginning of the year, a foreman has 7 dozen electric bulbs in stock. During the year, he receives a shipment of 14 dozen bulbs, and also replaces 5 burned out bulbs a month in each of 3 buildings in his area. How many electric bulbs does he have on hand at the end of the year? _______dozen. 8.____

A. 3 B. 6 C. 8 D. 12

9. A project has 4 buildings, each 14 floors high. Each floor has 10 apartments. If 35% of the apartments in the project have 3 rooms or less, how many apartments have 4 or more rooms? 9.____

A. 196 B. 210 C. 364 D. 406

10. An employee takes 1 hour and 30 minutes a day to sweep 30 flights of stairs. How many flights of stairs does he sweep in a month if he spends a total of 30 hours doing this job and works at the same rate? 10.____

A. 200 B. 300 C. 600 D. 900

11. During a month, Employee A washed 30 windows, Employee B washed 4 times as many windows as Employee A, and Employee C washed half as many windows as Employee B. The TOTAL number of windows washed by all three men together during this month is 11.____

A. 180 B. 210 C. 240 D. 330

12. How much would it cost to completely fence in the playground area shown at the right with fencing costing $7.50 a foot? 12.____

A. $615.00
B. $820.00
C. $885.00
D. $960.00

14FT.
9FT.
26FT.
33FT.

13. A drill bit measures .625 inches. The fractional equivalent, in inches, is 13.____

A. 9/16 B. 5/8 C. 11/16 D. 3/4

14. The number of cubic yards of sand required to fill a bin measuring 12 feet by 6 feet by 4 feet is MOST NEARLY 14.____

A. 8 B. 11 C. 48 D. 96

15. Assume that you are assigned to put down floor tiles in a room measuring 8 feet by 10 feet. Individual tiles measure 9 inches by 9 inches. The total number of floor tiles required to cover the entire floor is MOST NEARLY 15.____

A. 107 B. 121 C. 142 D. 160

16. Lumber is usually sold by the board foot, and a board foot is defined as a board one foot square and one inch thick. 16.____
If the price of one board foot of lumber is 90 cents and you need 20 feet of lumber 6 inches wide and 1 inch thick, the cost of the 20 feet of lumber is

A. $9.00 B. $12.00 C. $18.00 D. $24.00

17. For a certain plumbing repair job, you need three lengths of pipe, 12 1/4 inches, 6 1/2 inches, and 8 5/8 inches. 17.____
If you cut these three lengths from the same piece of pipe, which is 36 inches long, and each cut consumes 1/8 inch of pipe, the length of pipe REMAINING after you have cut out your three pieces should be _____ inches.

A. 7 1/4 B. 7 7/8 C. 8 1/4 D. 8 7/8

18. A maintenance bond for a roadway pavement is in an amount of 10% of the estimated cost. 18.____
If the estimated cost is $8,000,000, the maintenance bond is

A. $8,000 B. $80,000 C. $800,000 D. $8,000,000

19. Specifications require that a core be taken every 700 square yards of paved roadway or fraction thereof. A 100 foot by 200 foot rectangular area would require _____ core(s). 19.____

A. 1 B. 2 C. 3 D. 4

20. An applicant must file a map at a scale of 1" = 40'. Six inches on the map represents _____ feet on the ground. 20.____

A. 600 B. 240 C. 120 D. 60

21. A 100' x 110' lot has an area of MOST NEARLY _____ acre. 21.____

A. 1/8 B. 1/4 C. 3/8 D. 1/2

22. 1 inch is MOST NEARLY equal to _____ feet. 22.____

A. .02 B. .04 C. .06 D. .08

23. The area of the triangle EFG shown at the right is MOST NEARLY _____ sq. ft. 23.____

A. 36 B. 42 C. 48 D. 54

24. Specifications state: As further security for the faithful performance of this contract, the Comptroller shall deduct, and retain until the final payment, 10% of the value of the work certified for payment in each partial payment voucher, until the amount so deducted and retained shall equal 5% of the contract price or in the case of a unit price contract, 5% of the estimated amount to be paid to the Contractor under the contract. 24.____
For a $300,000 contract, the amount to be retained at the end of the contract is

A. $5,000 B. $10,000 C. $15,000 D. $20,000

25. Asphalt was laid for a length of 210 feet on the entire width of a street whose curb-to-curb distance is 30 feet. The number of square yards covered with asphalt is MOST NEARLY 25.____

A. 210 B. 700 C. 2,100 D. 6,300

KEY (CORRECT ANSWERS)

1. C
2. A
3. B
4. C
5. B
6. C
7. B
8. B
9. C
10. C
11. B
12. C
13. B
14. B
15. C
16. A
17. C
18. C
19. D
20. B
21. B
22. D
23. A
24. C
25. B

SOLUTIONS TO PROBLEMS

1. (2)(9) = 18 man-days. Then, 18 ÷ 3 = 6 men

2. The number of employees = 1644 ÷ 2 = 822. The number of foremen needed = 822 ÷ 18 ≈ 45

3. 1 gallon of wax costs the same as 60 ÷ 2 = 30 bars of soap. Thus, 5 gallons of wax costs the same as (5)(30) = 150 bars of soap.

4. To average 280 sq.ft. for five days means a total of (5)(280) = 1400 sq.ft. for all five days. The number of square feet to be waxed on Friday = 1400 - (275+352+179+302) = 292

5. The acreage for buildings is 35 - 28 = 7. Then, 7/35 = 20%

6. (16)(3/4) = 12 quarts = 3 gallons. The amount of detergent, in ounces, is (2)(3) = 6. The amount of disinfectant is 1 oz.

7. One corn broom weighs 32 ÷ 12 = 2 2/3 lbs. ≈ 2 lbs. 11 oz.

8. Number of bulbs at the beginning of the year = (7)(12) + (14)(12) = 252. Number of bulbs replaced over an entire year = (5)(3)(12) = 180. The number of unused bulbs = 252 - 180 = 72 = 6 dozen.

9. Total number of apartments = (4)(14)(10) = 560. The number of apartments with at least 4 rooms = (.65)(560) = 364.

10. 30 ÷ 1 1/2 = 20. Then, (20)(30) = 600 flights of stairs

11. The number of windows washed by A, B, C were 30, 120, and 60. Their total is 210.

12. The two missing dimensions are 26 - 14 = 12 ft. and 33 - 9 = 24 ft. Perimeter = 9 + 12 + 33 + 26 + 24 + 14 = 118 ft. Thus, total cost of fencing = (118)($7.50) = $885.00

13. $.625 = \frac{625}{1000} = \frac{5}{8}$

14. (12)(6)(4) = 288 cu.ft. Now, 1 cu.yd. = 27 cu.ft.; 288 cu.ft. is equivalent to 10 2/3 or about 11 cu.yds.

15. 144 sq.in. = 1 sq.ft. The room measures (8 ft.)x(10 ft.) = 80 sq.ft. = 11,520 sq.in. Each tile measures (9)(9) = 81 sq.in. The number of tiles needed = 11,520 ÷ 81 = 142.2 or about 142.

16. 20 ft. by 6 in. = (20 ft.)(1/2 ft.) = 10 sq.ft. Then, (10X.90) = $9.00

17. There will be 3 cuts in making 3 lengths of pipe, and these 3 cuts will use (3)(1/8) = 3/8 in. of pipe. The amount of pipe remaining after the 3 pieces are removed = 36 - 12 1/4 - 6 1/2 - 8 5/8 - 3/8 = 8 1/4 in.

18. The maintenance bond = (.10)($8,000,000) = $800,000

19. (100)(200) = 20,000 sq.ft. = 20,000 ÷ 9 ≈ 2222 sq.yds. Then, 2222 ÷ 700 ≈ 3.17. Since a core must be taken for each 700 sq.yds. plus any left over fraction, 4 cores will be needed.

20. Six inches means (6)(40) = 240 ft. of actual length.

21. (100 ft.)(110 ft.) = 11,000 sq.ft. ≈ 1222 sq.yds. Then, since 1 acre = 4840 sq.yds., 1222 sq.yds. is equivalent to about 1/4 acre.

22. 1 in. = 1/12 ft. ≈ .08 ft.

23. Area of Δ EFG = (1/2)(8)(6) + (1/2)(4)(6) = 36 sq.ft.

24. The amount to be retained = (.05)($300,000) = $15,000

25. (210)(30) = 6300 sq.ft. Since 1 sq.yd. = 9 sq.ft., 6300 sq.ft. equals 700 sq.yds.

TEST 2

DIRECTIONS: Each question or incomplete statement is followed by several suggested answers or completions. Select the one that BEST answers the question or completes the statement. *PRINT THE LETTER OF THE CORRECT ANSWER IN THE SPACE AT THE RIGHT.*

1. The TOTAL length of four pieces of 2" pipe, whose lengths are 7'3 1/2", 4'2 3/16", 5'7 5/16", and 8'5 7/8", respectively, is 1.____

   A. 24'6 3/4"
   B. 24'7 15/16"
   C. 25'5 13/16"
   D. 25'6 7/8"

2. Under the same conditions, the group of pipes that gives the SAME flow as one 6" pipe is (neglecting friction) ______ pipes. 2.____

   A. 3 3"
   B. 4 3"
   C. 2 4"
   D. 3 4"

3. A water storage tank measures 5' long, 4' wide, and 6' deep and is filled to the 5 1/2' mark with water. 3.____
   If one cubic foot of water weighs 62 pounds, the number of pounds of water required to COMPLETELY fill the tank is

   A. 7,440
   B. 6,200
   C. 1,240
   D. 620

4. A hot water line made of copper has a straight horizontal run of 150 feet and, when installed, is at a temperature of 45°F. In use, its temperature rises to 190°F. 4.____
   If the coefficient of expansion for copper is 0.0000095" per foot per degree F, the total expansion, in inches, in the run of pipe is given by the product of 150 multiplied by 0.0000095 by

   A. 145
   B. 145 x 12
   C. 145 divided by 12
   D. 145 x 12 x 12

5. To dig a trench 3'0" wide, 50'0" long, and 5'6" deep, the total number of cubic yards of earth to be removed Is MOST NEARLY 5.____

   A. 30
   B. 90
   C. 140
   D. 825

6. If it costs $65 for 20 feet of subway rail, the cost of 150 feet of this rail will be 6.____

   A. $487.50
   B. $512.00
   C. $589.50
   D. $650.00

7. The number of cubic feet of concrete it takes to fill a form 10 feet long, 3 feet wide, and 6 inches deep is 7.____

   A. 12
   B. 15
   C. 20
   D. 180

8. The sum of 4 1/16, 51/4, 3 5/8, and 4 7/16 is 8.____

   A. 17 3/16
   B. 17 1/4
   C. 17 5/16
   D. 17 3/8

9. If you earn $10.20 per hour and time and one-half for working over 40 hours, your gross salary for a week in which you worked 42 hours would be 9.____

   A. $408.00
   B. $428.40
   C. $438.60
   D. $770.80

10. A drill bit, used to drill holes in track ties, has a diameter of 0.75 inches. When expressed as a fraction, the diameter of this drill bit is 10.____

A. 1/4" B. 3/8" C. 1/2" D. 3/4"

11. Three dozen shovels were purchased for use. If the shovels were used at the rate of nine a week, the number of weeks that the three dozen lasted was 11.____

A. 3 B. 4 C. 9 D. 12

12. Assume that you earn $20,000 per year. If twenty percent of your pay is deducted for taxes, social security, and pension, your weekly take-home pay will be MOST NEARLY 12.____

A. $280 B. $308 C. $328 D. $344

13. If a measurement scaled from a drawing is one inch, and the scale of the drawing is 1/8 inch to the foot, then the one inch measurement would represent an ACTUAL length of 13.____

A. 8 feet B. 2 feet
C. 1/8 of a foot D. 8 inches

14. Tiles 12" x 12" are used to lay a floor having the dimensions 10'0" x 12'0". The MINIMUM number of tiles needed to completely cover the floor is 14.____

A. 60 B. 96 C. 120 D. 144

15. The volume of concrete in a strip of sidewalk 30 feet long by 4 feet wide by 3 inches thick is _____ cubic feet. 15.____

A. 30 B. 120 C. 240 D. 360

16. To change a quantity of cubic feet into an equivalent quantity of cubic yards, _____ the quantity by _____. 16.____

A. multiply; 9 B. divide; 9
C. multiply; 27 D. divide; 27

17. If a pump can deliver 50 gallons of water per minute, then the time needed for this pump to empty an excavation containing 5,800 gallons of water is _____ hour(s) _____ minutes. 17.____

A. 2; 12 B. 1; 56 C. 1; 44 D. 1; 32

18. The sum of 3 1/6", 4 1/4", 3 5/8", and 5 7/16" is 18.____

A. 15 9/16" B. 16 1/8" C. 16 23/48" D. 16 3/4"

19. If a measurement scaled from a drawing is 2 inches, and the scale of the drawing is 1/8 inch to the foot, then the two inch measurement would represent an ACTUAL length of 19.____

A. 8 feet B. 4 feet
C. 1/4 of a foot D. 16 feet

20. A room is 7'6" wide by 9'0" long with a ceiling height of 8'0". One gallon of flat paint will cover approximately 400 square feet of wall. The number of gallons of this paint required to paint the walls of this room, making no deductions for windows or doors, is MOST NEARLY 20.____

A. 1/4 B. 1/2 C. 2/3 D. 1

21. The cost of a certain job is broken down as follows: 21.____

Materials	$3,750
Rental of equipment	1,200
Labor	3,150

The percentage of the total cost of the job that can be charged to materials is MOST NEARLY

A. 40% B. 42% C. 44% D. 46%

22. By trial, it is found that by using two cubic feet of sand, a 5 cubic foot batch of concrete is produced. Using the same proportions, the amount of sand required to produce 2 cubic yards of concrete is MOST NEARLY _____ cubic feet. 22.____

A. 20 B. 22 C. 24 D. 26

23. It takes 4 men 6 days to do a certain job. Working at the same speed, the number of days it will take 3 men to do this job is 23.____

A. 7 B. 8 C. 9 D. 10

24. The cost of rawl plugs is $27.50 per gross. The cost of 2,448 rawl plugs is 24.____

A. $467.50 B. $472.50 C. $477.50 D. $482.50

25. In a certain district, the area of a building may be no longer than 55% of the area of the lot on which it stands. On a rectangular lot 75 ft. by 125 ft., the maximum permissible area of building is, in square feet, MOST NEARLY 25.____

A. 5,148 B. 5,152 C. 5,156 D. 5,160

KEY (CORRECT ANSWERS)

1. D
2. B
3. D
4. A
5. A
6. A
7. B
8. D
9. C
10. D
11. B
12. B
13. A
14. C
15. A
16. D
17. B
18. C
19. D
20. C
21. D
22. B
23. B
24. A
25. C

SOLUTIONS TO PROBLEMS

1. $3\frac{1}{6}"+4\frac{1}{4}"+3\frac{5}{8}"+5\frac{7}{16}"+=3\frac{8}{48}"+4\frac{12}{48}"+3\frac{30}{48}"+5\frac{21}{48}"=15\frac{71}{48}"=16\frac{23}{48}"$

2. The flow of a 6" pipe is measured by the cross-sectional area. Since diameter = 6", radius = 3", and so area = 9 π sq.in. A single 3" pipe would have a cross-sectional area of (3/2) π sq.in. = 2.25 π sq.in. Now, 9 ÷ / 2.25 = 4. Thus, four 3" pipes is equivalent, in flow, to one 6" pipe.

3. (5x4x6) - (5x4x5 1/2) = 10. Then, (10)(62) = 620 pounds.

4. The total expansion = (150')(.0000095"/1 ft.)(190°-45°). So, the last factor is 145.

5. (3')(50')(5 1/2') = 825 cu.ft. Since 1 cu.yd. = 27 cu.ft., 825 cu.ft. cu.yds.

6. 150 ÷ 20 = 7.5. Then, (7.5)($65) = $487.50

7. (10')(3')(1/2') = 15 cu.ft.

8. $4\frac{1}{16}+5\frac{4}{16}+3\frac{10}{16}+4\frac{7}{16}=16\frac{22}{16}=17\frac{3}{8}$

9. Gross salary = ($10.20)(40) + ($15.30)(2) = $438.60

10. $75"=\frac{75}{100}"=\frac{3}{4}"$

11. 3 dozen = 36 shovels. Then, 36 ÷ 9 = 4 weeks

12. Since 20% is deducted, the take-home pay = ($20,000)(.80) = $16,000 for the year, which is $16,000 ÷ 52 ≈ $308 per week.

13. A scale drawing where 1/8" means an actual size of 1 ft. implies that a scale drawing of 1" means an actual size of (1')(8) = 8'

14. (10')(12') = 120 sq.ft. Since each tile is 1 sq.ft., a total of 120 tiles will be used.

15. (30')(4')(1/4') = 30 cu.ft.

16. To convert a given number of cubic feet into an equivalent number of cubic yards, divide by 27.

17. 5800 ÷ 50 = 116 min. = 1 hour 56 minutes

18. $3\frac{1}{6}"+4\frac{1}{4}"+3\frac{5}{8}"+5\frac{7}{16}"+=3\frac{8}{48}"+4\frac{12}{48}"+3\frac{30}{48}"+5\frac{21}{48}"=15\frac{71}{48}"=16\frac{23}{48}"$

19. 2 ÷ 1/8 = 16, so a 2" drawing represents an actual length of 16 feet.

20. The area of the 4 walls = 2(7 1/2')(8') + 2(9')(8') = 264 sq.ft. Then, 264 ÷ 400 = .66 or about 2/3 gallon of paint.

21. $3750 + $1200 + $3150 = $8100. Then, $3750/$8100 ≈ 46%

22. 2 cu.yds. ÷ 5 cu.ft. = 54 ÷ 5 = 10.8. Now, (10.8)(2 cu.ft.) ≈ 22 cu.ft. Note: 2 cu.yds. = 54 cu.ft.

23. (4)(6) = 24 man-days. Then, 24 ÷ 3 = 8 days

24. 2448 ÷ 144 = 17. Then, (17)($27.50) = $467.50

25. (75')(125') = 9375 sq.ft. The maximum area of the building = (.55)(9375 sq.ft.) * 5156 sq.ft.

TEST 3

DIRECTIONS: Each question or incomplete statement is followed by several suggested answers or completions. Select the one that BEST answers the question or completes the statement. *PRINT THE LETTER OF THE CORRECT ANSWER IN THE SPACE AT THE RIGHT.*

1. A steak weighed 2 pounds, 4 ounces. 1.____
How much did it cost at $4.60 per pound?

   A. $7.80 B. $8.75 C. $9.90 D. $10.35

2. twenty pints of water just fill a pail. 2.____
the capacity of the pail, in gallons, is

   A. 2 B. 2 1/4 C. 2 1/2 D. 2 3/4

3. The sum of 5/12 and 1/4 is 3.____

   A. 7/12 B. 2/3 C. 3/4 D. 5/6

4. The volume of earth, in cubic yards, excavated from a trench 4'0" wide by 5'6" deep by 18'6" long is MOST NEARLY 4.____

   A. 14.7 B. 15.1 C. 15.5 D. 15.9

5. 5/8 written as a decimal is 5.____

   A. 62.5 B. 6.25 C. .625 D. .0625

6. The number of cubic feet in a cubic yard is 6.____

   A. 9 B. 12 C. 27 D. 36

7. If it costs $16.20 to lay one square yard of asphalt, to lay a patch 15' by 15', it will cost MOST NEARLY 7.____

   A. $405.00 B. $3,645.00 C. $134.50 D. $243.00

8. You are assigned thirty (30) asphalt workers to be divided into two crews so that one crew will have 2/3 as many men as the other. 8.____
The number of men you would put into the SMALLER crew is

   A. 10 B. 12 C. 14 D. 20

9. It takes 12 asphalt workers, working 6 hours a day, 5 days to complete a certain job. 9.____
The number of days it will take 10 men, working 8 hours a day, to do the same job, assuming all work at the same rate, is

   A. 2 1/2 B. 3 C. 4 1/2 D. 6

0. A street is laid to a 3% grade. 10.____
This means that in 150 ft., the street grade will rise

   A. 4 1/2 inches B. 45 inches
   C. 4 1/2 feet D. 45 feet

11. The sum of the following dimensions, 3 4/8, 4 1/8, 5 1/8, and 6 1/4, is 11.____

A. 19 B. 19 1/8 C. 19 1/4 D. 19 1/2

12. A worker is paid $9.30 per hour. 12.____
If he works 8 hours each day on Monday, Tuesday, and Wednesday, 3 1/2 hours on Thursday, and 3 hours on Friday, the TOTAL amount due him is

A. $283.65 B. $289.15 C. $276.20 D. $285.35

13. The price of metal lath is $395.00 per 100 square yards. The cost of 527 square yards of this lath is MOST NEARLY 13.____

A. $2,076.50 B. $2,079.10 C. $2,081.70 D. $2,084.30

14. The total cost of applying 221 square yards of plaster board is $3,430. 14.____
The cost per square yard is MOST NEARLY

A. $14.00 B. $14.50 C. $15.00 D. $15.50

15. In a three-coat plaster job, the scratch coat is 1/8 in. thick in front of the lath, the brown coat is 3/16 in. thick, and the finish coat is 1/8 in. thick. 15.____
The TOTAL thickness of this plaster job, measured from the face of the lath, is

A. 7/16" B. 1/2" C. 9/16" D. 5/8"

16. If an asphalt worker earns $38,070 per year, his wages per month are MOST NEARLY 16.____

A. $380.70 B. $735.00 C. $3,170.00 D. $3,807.00

17. The sum of 4 1/2 inches, 3 1/4 inches, and 7 1/2 inches is 1 foot _____ inches. 17.____

A. 3 B. 3 1/4 C. 3 1/2 D. 4

18. The area of a rectangular asphalt patch, 9 ft. 3 in. by 6 ft. 9 in., is _____ square feet. 18.____

A. 54 B. 54 1/4 C. 54 1/2 D. 62 7/16

19. The number of cubic feet in a cubic yard is 19.____

A. 3 B. 9 C. 16 D. 27

20. A 450 ft. long street with a grade of 2% will have one end of the street higher than the other end by _____ feet. 20.____

A. 2 B. 44 C. 9 D. 20

21. If the drive wheel of a roller is 6 ft. in diameter and the tiller wheel is 4 ft. in diameter, whenever the drive wheel makes a complete revolution on a straight pass, the tiller wheel makes _____ revolution(s). 21.____

A. 1 B. 1 1/4 C. 1 1/2 D. 2

22. A point on the centerline of a street is marked: Station 42 + 51. Another point on the centerline 30 feet from the first is marked Station 42+81. 22.____
A third should be marked Station

A. 12+51 B. 42+21 C. 45+51 D. 72+51

23. In twenty minutes, a truck moving with a speed of 30 miles an hour will cover a distance of _____ miles. 23.____

A. 3 B. 5 C. 10 D. 30

24. The number of pounds in a ton is 24.____

A. 500 B. 1,000 C. 2,000 D. 5,000

25. During his summer vacation, a boy earned $45.00 per day and saved 60% of his earnings. 25.____
If he worked 45 days, how much did he save during his vacation?

A. $15.00 B. $18.00 C. $1,215.00 D. $22.50

KEY (CORRECT ANSWERS)

1. D
2. C
3. B
4. B
5. C

6. C
7. A
8. B
9. C
10. C

11. A
12. A
13. C
14. D
15. A

16. C
17. B
18. D
19. D
20. C

21. C
22. B
23. C
24. C
25. C

SOLUTIONS TO PROBLEMS

1. ($4.60)(2 1/4 lbs.) = $10.35

2. 1 gallon = 8 pints, so 20 pints = 20/8 = 2 1/2 gallons

3. $\frac{5}{12}+\frac{1}{4}=\frac{5}{12}+\frac{3}{12}=\frac{8}{12}=\frac{2}{3}$

4. (4')(5 1/2')(18 1/2') = 407 cu.ft. Since 1 cu.yd. = 27 cu.ft., 407 cu.ft. ≈ 15.1 cu.yds.

5. 5/8=5 ÷ 8.000 = .625

6. There are (3)(3)(3) =27 cu.ft. in a cu.yd.

7. (15')(15') = 225 sq.ft. = 25 sq.yds. Then, ($16.20)(25) = $405.00

8. Let 2x = size of smaller crew and 3x = size of larger crew. Then, 2x + 3x = 30. Solving, x = 6. Thus, the smaller crew consists of 12 workers.

9. (12)(6)(5) = 360 worker-days. Then, 360 ÷ [(10)(8)] = 4 1/2 days

10. (.03)(150') = 4 1/2 ft.

11. $3\frac{4}{8}+4\frac{1}{8}+5\frac{1}{8}+6\frac{2}{8}=18\frac{8}{8}=19$

12. ($9.30)(8+8+8+3 1/2+3) = ($9.30)(30 1/2) = $283.65

13. The cost of 527 sq.yds. = (5.27)($395.00) = $2081.65 ≈ $2081.70

14. $3430 ÷ 221 ≈ $15.50

15. $\frac{1}{8}"+\frac{3}{16}"+\frac{1}{8}"=\frac{2}{16}"+\frac{3}{16}"+\frac{2}{16}"=\frac{7}{16}"$

16. $38,070 ÷ 12 = $3172.50 ≈ $3170.00 per month

17. 4 1/2" + 3 1/4" + 7 1/2" = 15 1/4" = 1 ft. 3 1/4 in.

18. 9 ft. 3 in. = 9 1/4 ft., 6 ft. 9 in. = 6 3/4 ft. Area = (9 1/4) (6 3/4) = 62 7/16 sq.ft.

19. A cubic yard = (3)(3)(3) = 27 cubic feet

20. (450')(.02) = 9 ft.

21. 6/4 = 1 1/2 revolutions

22. Station 42 + 51
    30 ft away would be 51 + 30 = 81 OR 51 - 30 = 21
    Station 42 + 81 or 42 + 21 (ANSWER: B)

23. 30 miles in 60 minutes means 10 miles in 20 minutes.

24. There are 2000 pounds in a ton.

25. ($45.00)(.60) = $27.00 savings per day. For 45 days, his savings is (45)($27.00) = $1215.00

BASIC FUNDAMENTALS OF
DRAWINGS AND SPECIFICATIONS

A building project may be broadly divided into two major phases: (1) the DESIGN phase, and (2) the CONSTRUCTION phase. In accordance with a number of considerations, of which the function and desired appearance of the building are perhaps the most important, the architect first conceives the building in his mind's eye, as it were, and then sets his concept down on paper in the form of PRESENTATION drawings. Presentation drawings are usually done in PERSPECTIVE, by employing the PICTORIAL drawing techniques.

Next the architect and the engineer, working together, decide upon the materials to be used in the structure and the construction methods which are to be followed. The engineer determines the loads which supporting members will carry and the strength qualities the members must have to bear the loads. He also designs the mechanical systems of the structure, such as the lighting, heating, and plumbing systems. The end-result of all this is the preparation of architectural and engineering DESIGN SKETCHES. The purpose of these sketches is to guide draftsmen in the preparation of CONSTRUCTION DRAWINGS.

The construction drawings, plus the SPECIFICATIONS to be described later, are the chief sources of information for the supervisors and craftsman responsible for the actual work of construction. Construction drawings consist mostly of ORTHOGRAPHIC views, prepared by draftsmen who employ the standard technical drawing techniques, and who use the symbols and other designations

You should make a thorough study of symbols before proceeding further with this chapter. Figure 1 illustrates the conventional symbols for the more common types of material used on structures. Figure 2 shows the more common symbols used for doors and windows.

Before you can interpret construction drawings correctly, you must also have some knowledge of the structure and of the terminology for common structural members.

I. STRUCTURES

The main parts of a structure are the LOAD-BEARING STRUCTURAL MEMBERS, which support and transfer the loads on the structure while remaining in equilibrium with each other. The places where members are connected to other members are called JOINTS. The sum total of the load supported by the structural members at a particular instant is equal to the total DEAD LOAD plus the total LIVE LOAD.

The total dead load is the total weight of the structure, which gradually increases, of course, as the structure rises, and remains constant once it is completed. The total live load is the total weight of movable objects (such as people, furniture, bridge traffic or the like) which the structure happens to be supporting at a particular instant.

The live loads in a structure are transmitted through the various load-bearing structural members to the ultimate support of the earth as follows. Immediate or direct support for the live loads is provided by HORIZTONAL members; these are in turn supported by VERTICAL members; which in turn are supported by FOUNDATIONS and/or FOOTINGS; and these are, finally, supported by the earth.

The ability of the earth to support a load is called the SOIL BEARING CAPACITY; it is determined by test and measured in pounds per square foot. Soil bearing capacity varies considerably with different types of soil, and a soil of given bearing capacity will bear a heavier load on a wide foundation or footing than it will on a narrow one.

VERTICAL STRUCTURAL MEMBERS

Vertical structural members are high-strength columns; they are sometimes called PILLARS in buildings. Outside wall columns and inside bottom-floor columns, usually rest directly on footings. Outside-wall columns usually extend from the footing or foundation to the roof line. Inside bottom-floor columns extend upward from footings or foundations to horizontal members which in turn support the

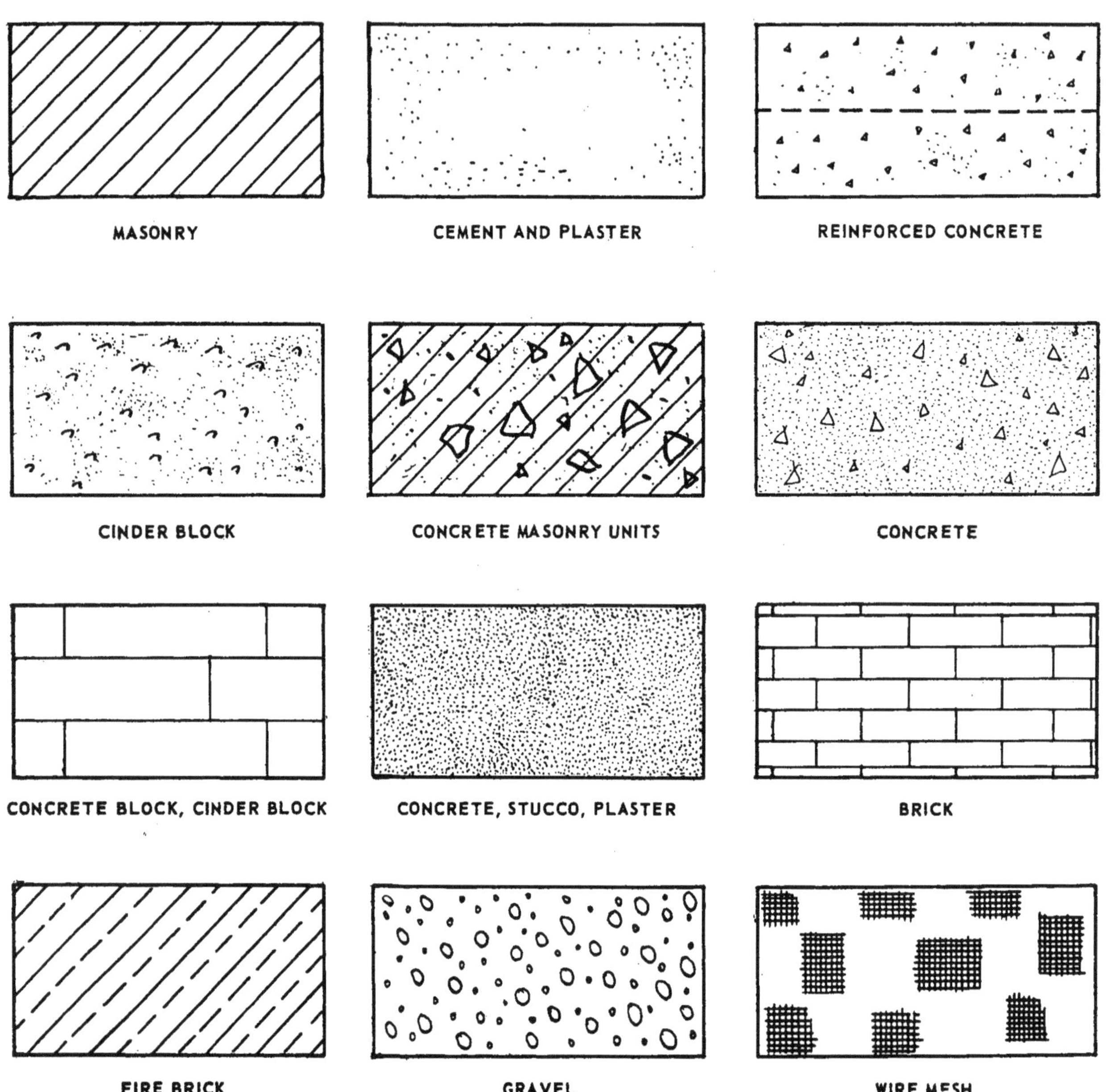

Figure 1.—Material symbols.

first floor. Upper floor columns usually are located directly over lower floor columns.

A PIER in building construction might be called a short column. It may rest directly on a footing, or it may be simply set or driven in the ground. Building piers usually support the lowermost horizontal structural members.

In bridge construction a pier is a vertical member which provides intermediate support for the bridge superstructure.

The chief vertical structural members in light frame construction are called STUDS. They are supported on horizontal members called SILLS or SOLE PLATES, and are topped by horizontal members called TOP PLATES or RAFTER PLATES. CORNER POSTS are enlarged studs, as it were, located at the building corners. In early FULL-FRAME construction a corner post was usually a solid piece of larger timber. In most modern construction BUILT-UP

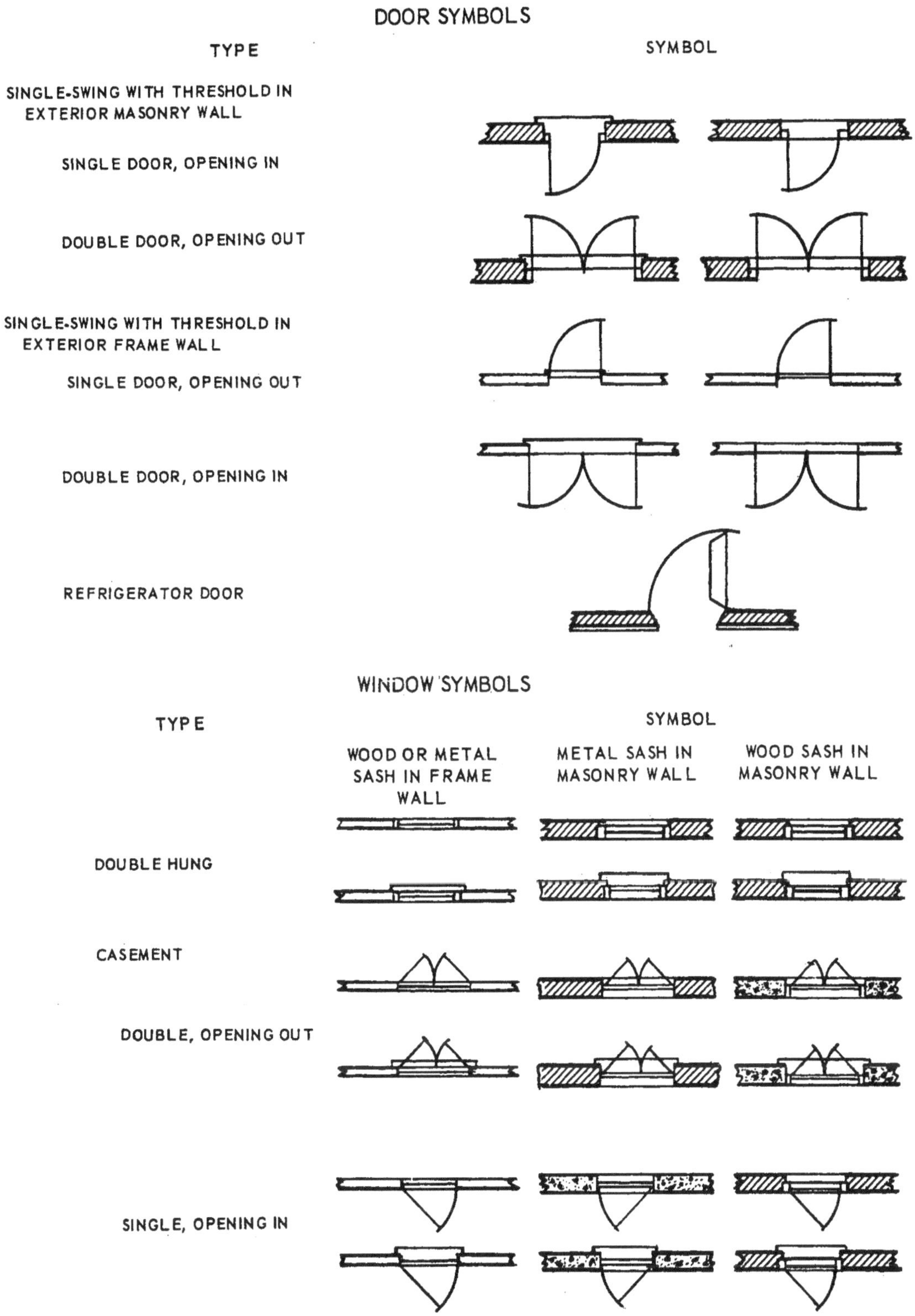

DOOR SYMBOLS

TYPE	SYMBOL
SINGLE-SWING WITH THRESHOLD IN EXTERIOR MASONRY WALL	
SINGLE DOOR, OPENING IN	
DOUBLE DOOR, OPENING OUT	
SINGLE-SWING WITH THRESHOLD IN EXTERIOR FRAME WALL	
SINGLE DOOR, OPENING OUT	
DOUBLE DOOR, OPENING IN	
REFRIGERATOR DOOR	

WINDOW SYMBOLS

TYPE	SYMBOL		
	WOOD OR METAL SASH IN FRAME WALL	METAL SASH IN MASONRY WALL	WOOD SASH IN MASONRY WALL
DOUBLE HUNG			
CASEMENT			
DOUBLE, OPENING OUT			
SINGLE, OPENING IN			

Figure 2 —Architectural symbols (door and windows).

corner posts are used, consisting of various numbers of ordinary studs, nailed together in various ways.

HORIZONTAL STRUCTURAL MEMBERS

In technical terminology, a horizontal load-bearing structural member which spans a space, and which is supported at both ends, is called a BEAM. A member which is FIXED at one end only is called a CANTILEVER. Steel members which consist of solid pieces of the regular structural steel shapes are called beams, but a type of steel member which is actually a light truss is called an OPEN-WEB STEEL JOIST or a BAR STEEL JOIST.

Horizontal structural members which support the ends of floor beams or joists in wood frame construction are called SILLS, GIRTS, or GIRDERS, depending on the type of framing being done and the location of the member in the structure. Horizontal members which support studs are called SILL or SOLE PLATES. Horizontal members which support the wall-ends of rafters are called RAFTER PLATES. Horizontal members which assume the weight of concrete or masonry walls above door and window openings are called LINTELS.

TRUSSES

A beam of given strength,. without intermediate supports below, can support a given load over only a certain maximum span. If the span is wider than this maximum, intermediate supports, such as a column must be provided for the beam. Sometimes it is not feasible or possible to install intermediate supports. When such is the case, a TRUSS may be used instead of a beam.

A beam consists of a single horizontal member. A truss, however, is a framework, consisting of two horizontal (or nearly horizontal) members, joined together by a number of vertical and/or inclined members. The horizontal members are called the UPPER and LOWER CHORDS; the vertical and/or inclined members are called the WEB MEMBERS.

ROOF MEMBERS

The horizontal or inclined members which provide support to a roof are called RAFTERS. The lengthwise (right angle to the rafters) member which support the peak ends of the rafters in a roof is called the RIDGE. (The ridge may be called the Ridge board, the Ridge PIECE, or the Ridge pole.) Lengthwise members other than ridges are called PURLINS. In wood frame construction the wall ends of rafters are supported on horizontal members called RAFTER PLATES, which are in turn supported by the outside wall studs. In concrete or masonry wall construction, the wall ends of rafters may be anchored directly on the walls, or on plates bolted to the walls.

II. CONSTRUCTION DRAWINGS

Construction drawings are drawings in which as much construction information as possible is presented GRAPHICALLY, or by means of pictures. Most construction drawings consist of ORTHOGRAPHIC views. GENERAL drawings consist of PLANS AND ELEVATIONS, drawn on a relatively small scale. DETAIL drawings consist of SECTIONS and DETAILS, drawn on a relatively large scale.

PLANS

A PLAN view is, as you know, a view of an object or area as it would appear if projected onto a horizontal plane passed through or held above the object or area. The most common construction plans are PLOT PLANS (also called SITE PLANS), FOUNDATION PLANS, FLOOR PLANS, and FRAMING PLANS.

A PLOT PLAN shows the contours, boundaries, roads, utilities, trees, structures, and any other significant physical features pertaining to or located on the site. The locations of proposed structures are indicated by appropriate outlines or floor plans. By locating the corners of a proposed structure at given distances from a REFERENCE or BASE line (which is shown on the plan and which can be located on the site), the plot plan provides essential data for those who will lay out the building lines. By indicating the elevations of existing and proposed earth surfaces (by means of CONTOUR lines), the plot plan provides essential data for the graders and excavators.

A FOUNDATION PLAN (fig. 3) is a plan view of a structure projected on a horizontal plane passed through (in imagination, of course) at the level of the tops of the foundations. The plan shown in figure 3 tells you that the main foundation of this structure will consist of a rectangular 12-in. concrete block wall, 22 ft

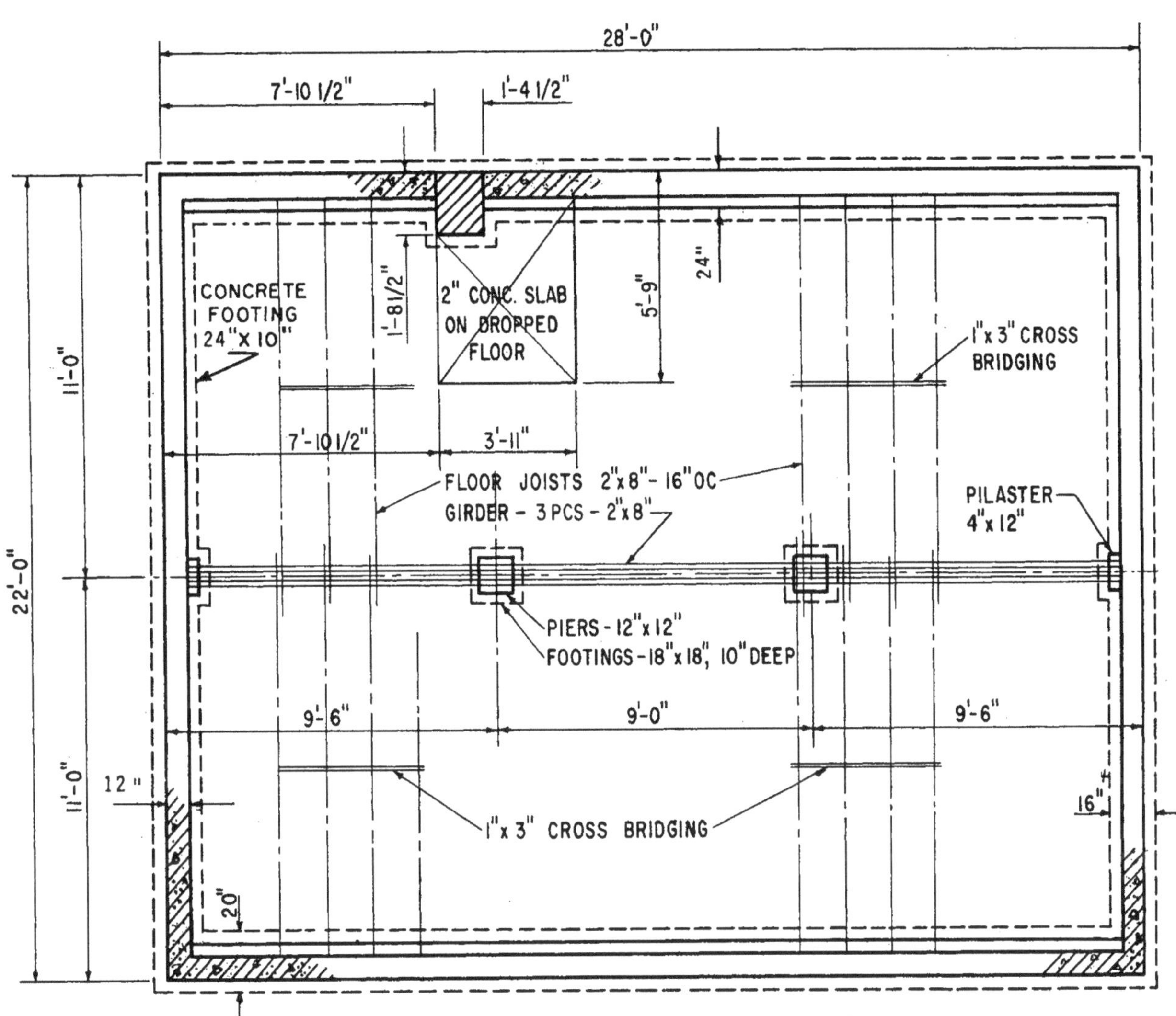

Figure 3.—Foundation plan.

wide by 28 ft long, centered on a concrete footing 24 in. wide. Besides the outside wall and footing, there will be two 12-in. square piers, centered on 18-in. square footings, and located on center 9 ft 6 in. from the end wall building lines. These piers will support a ground floor center-line girder.

A FLOOR PLAN (also called a BUILDING PLAN) is developed as shown in figure 4. Information on a floor plan includes the lengths, thicknesses, and character of the building walls at that particular floor, the widths and locations of door and window openings, the lengths and character of partitions, the number and arrangement of rooms, and the types and locations of utility installations. A typical floor plan is shown in figure 5.

FRAMING PLANS show the dimensions, numbers, and arrangement of structural members in wood frame construction. A simple FLOOR FRAMING PLAN is superimposed on the foundation plan shown in figure 3. From this foundation plan you learn that the ground-floor joists in this structure will consist of 2 x 8's, lapped at the girder, and spaced 16 in. O. C. The plan also shows that each row of joists is to be braced by a row of 1 x 3 cross bridging. For a more complicated floor framing problem, a framing plan like the one shown in figure 2-6 would be required. This plan

PERSPECTIVE VIEW OF A BUILDING SHOWING CUTTING PLANE WXY

PREVIOUS PERSPECTIVE VIEW AT CUTTING PLANE WXYZ, TOP REMOVED

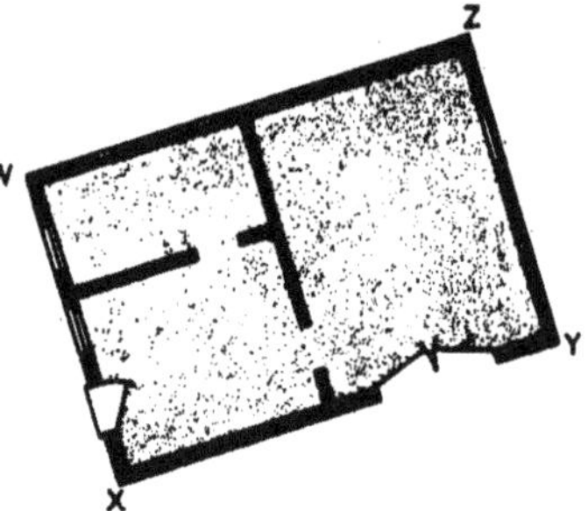

DEVELOPED FLOOR PLAN WXYZ

Figure 4.—Floor plan development.

shows, among other things, the arrangement of joists and other members around stair wells and other floor openings.

A WALL FRAMING PLAN gives similar information with regard to the studs, corner posts, bracing, sills, plates, and other structural members in the walls. Since it is a view on a vertical plane, a wall framing plan is not a plan in the strict technical sense. However, the practice of calling it a plan has become a general custom. A ROOF FRAMING PLAN gives similar information with regard to the rafters, ridge, purlins, and other structural members in the roof.

A UTILITY PLAN is a floor plan which shows the layout of a heating, electrical, plumbing, or other utility system. Utility plans are used primarily by the ratings responsible for the utilities, but they are important to the Builder as well. Most utility installations require the leaving of openings in walls, floors, and roofs for the admission or installation of utility features. The Builder who is placing a concrete foundation wall must study the utility plans to determine the number, sizes, and locations of the openings he must leave for utilities.

Figure 7 shows a heating plan. Figure 8 shows an electrical plan.

ELEVATIONS

ELEVATIONS show the front, rear, and sides of a structure projected on vertical planes parallel to the planes of the sides. Front, rear, right side, and left side elevations of a small building are shown in figure 9.

As you can see, the elevations give you a number of important vertical dimensions, such as the perpendicular distance from the finish floor to the top of the rafter plate and from the finish floor to the tops of door and window finished openings. They also show the locations and characters of doors and windows. Dimensions of window sash and dimensions and character of lintels, however, are usually set forth in a WINDOW SCHEDULE.

A SECTION view is a view of a cross-section, developed as indicated in figure 10. By general custom, the term is confined to views of cross-sections cut by vertical planes. A floor plan or foundation plan, cut by a horizontal plane, is, technically speaking, a section view as well as a plan view, but it is seldom called a section.

The most important sections are the WALL sections. Figure 11 shows three wall sections for three alternate types of construction for the building shown in figures 3, 5, 7 and 8. The angled arrows marked "A" in figure 5 indicate the location of the cutting plane for the sections.

The wall sections are of primary importance to the supervisors of construction and to the craftsmen who will do the actual building. Take the first wall section, marked "masonry construction," for example. Starting at the bottom, you learn that the footing will be concrete, 2 ft wide and 10 in. high. The vertical distance of the bottom of the footing below FINISHED GRADE (level of the finished earth surface around the house) "varies"—meaning that it will depend on the soil-bearing capacity at the particular site. The foundation wall will consist of

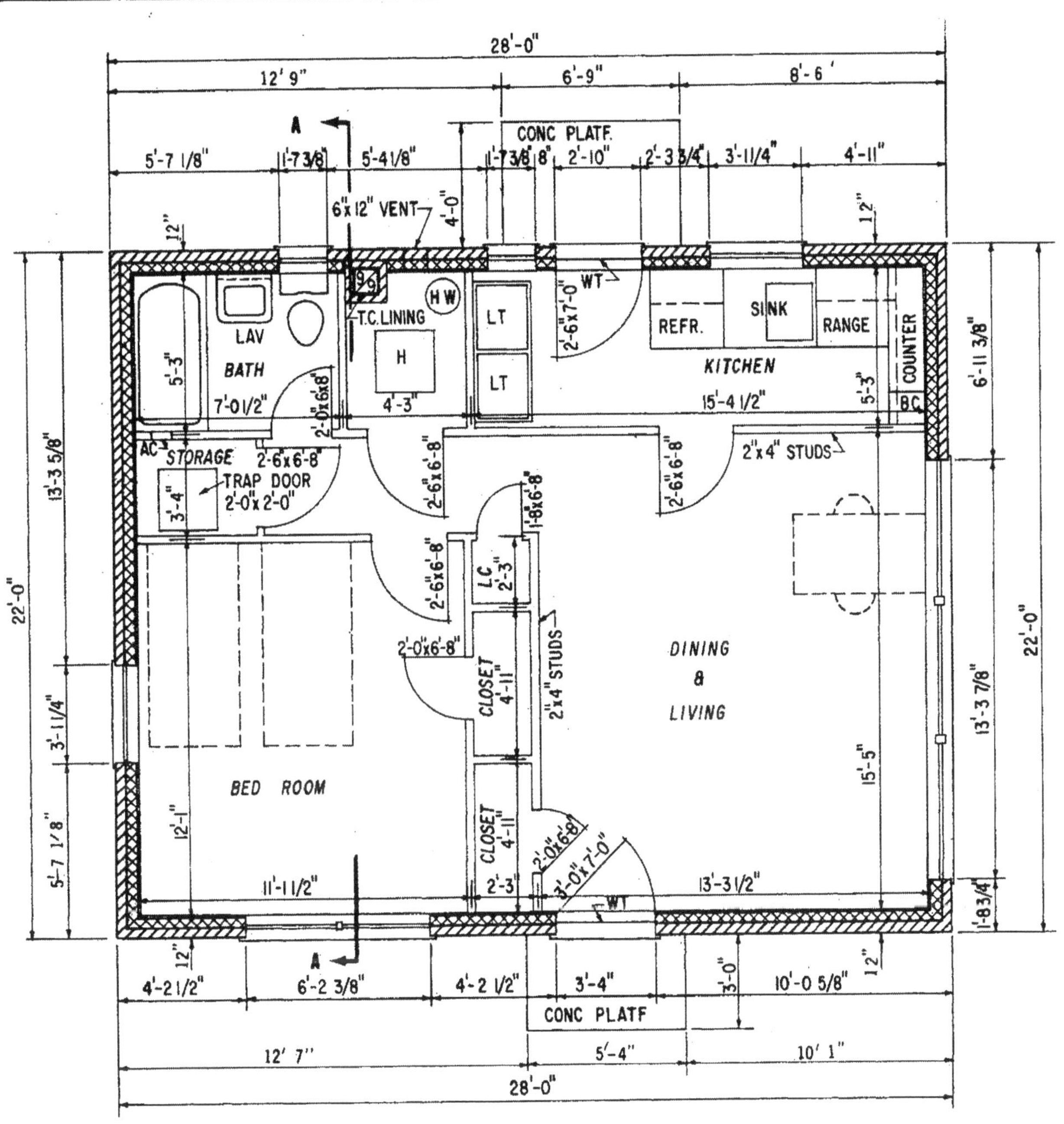

Figure 5.—Floor plan.

12-in. CMU, centered on the footing. Twelve-inch blocks will extend up to an unspecified distance below grade, where a 4-in. brick FACING (dimension indicated in the middle wall section) begins. Above the line of the bottom of the facing, it is obvious that 8-in. instead of 12-in. blocks will be used in the foundation wall.

The building wall above grade will consist of a 4-in. brick FACING TIER, backed by a BACKING TIER of 4-in. cinder blocks. The floor joists, consisting of 2 x 8's placed 16 in. O.C., will be anchored on 2 x 4 sills bolted to the top of the foundation wall. Every third joist will be additionally secured by a 2 x 1/4 STRAP ANCHOR embedded in the cinder block backing tier of the building wall.

The window (window B in the plan front elevation, fig. 9) will have a finished opening

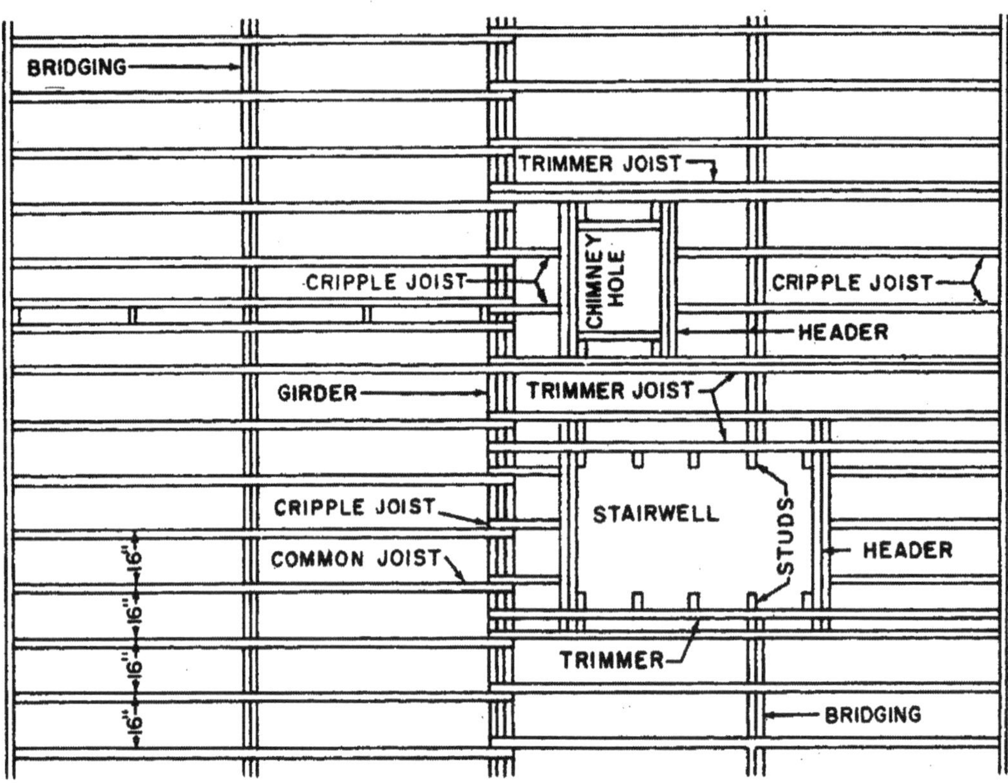

Figure . ·6.—Floor framing plan.

4 ft 2-5/8 in. high. The bottom of the opening will come 2 ft 11-3/4 in. above the line of the finished floor. As indicated in the wall section, (fig. 11) 13 masonry COURSES (layers of masonry units) above the finished floor line will amount to a vertical distance of 2 ft 11-3/4 in. As also indicated, another 19 courses will amount to the prescribed vertical dimension of the finished window opening.

Window framing details, including the placement and cross-sectional character of the lintel, are shown. The building wall will be carried 10-1/4 in., less the thickness of a 2 x 8 RAFTER PLATE, above the top of the window finished opening. The total vertical distance from the top of the finished floor to the top of the rafter plate will be 8 ft 2-1/4 in. Ceiling joists and rafters will consist of 2 x 6's, and the roof covering will consist of composition shingles laid on wood sheathing.

Flooring will consist of a wood finisher floor laid on a wood subfloor. Inside walls will be finished with plaster on lath (except on masonry wall which would be with or without lath as directed). A minimum of 2 vertical feet of crawl space will extend below the bottoms of the floor joists.

The middle wall section in figure 2-11 gives you similar information for a similar building constructed with wood frame walls and a DOUBLE-HUNG window. The third wall section shown in the figure gives you similar information for a similar building constructed with a steel frame, a casement window, and a concrete floor finished with asphalt tile.

DETAILS

DETAIL drawings are drawings which are done on a larger scale than that of the general drawings, and which show features not appearing at all, or appearing on too small a scale, on the general drawings. The wall sections just described are details as well as sections, since

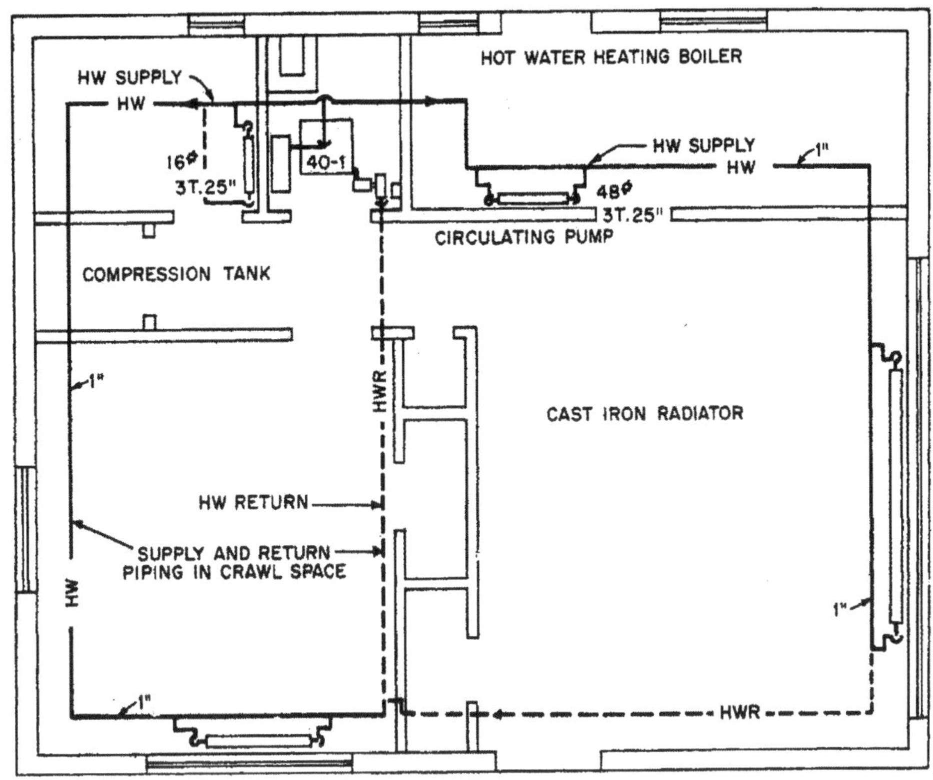

Figure 7.—Heating plan.

they are drawn on a considerable larger scale than the plans and elevations. Framing details at doors, windows, and cornices, which are the most common types of details, are practically always sections.

Details are included whenever the information given in the plans, elevations, and wall sections is not sufficiently "detailed" to guide the craftsmen on the job. Figure 12 shows some typical door and window wood framing details, and an eave detail for a very simple type of CORNICE. You should study these details closely to learn the terminology of framing members.

III. SPECIFICATIONS

The construction drawings contain much of the information about a structure which can be presented GRAPHICALLY (that is, in drawings). A very considerable amount of information can be presented this way, but there is more information which the construction supervisors and artisans must have and which is not adaptable to the graphic form of presentation. Information of this kind includes quality criteria for materials (maximum amounts of aggregate per sack of cement, for example), specified standards of workmanship, prescribed construction methods, and the like.

Information of this kind is presented in a list of written SPECIFICATIONS, familiarly known as the "SPECS." A list of specifications usually begins with a section on GENERAL CONDITIONS. This section starts with a GENERAL DESCRIPTION of the building, including the type of foundation, type or types of windows, character of framing, utilities to be installed, and the like. Next comes a list of DEFINITIONS of terms used in the specs, and next certain routine declarations of responsibility and certain conditions to be maintained on the job.

SPECIFIC CONDITIONS are grouped in sections under headings which describe each of the major construction phases of the job. Separate specifications are written for each phase, and the phases are then combined to more or less follow the usual order of construction sequences on the job. A typical list of sections under "Specific Conditions" follows:

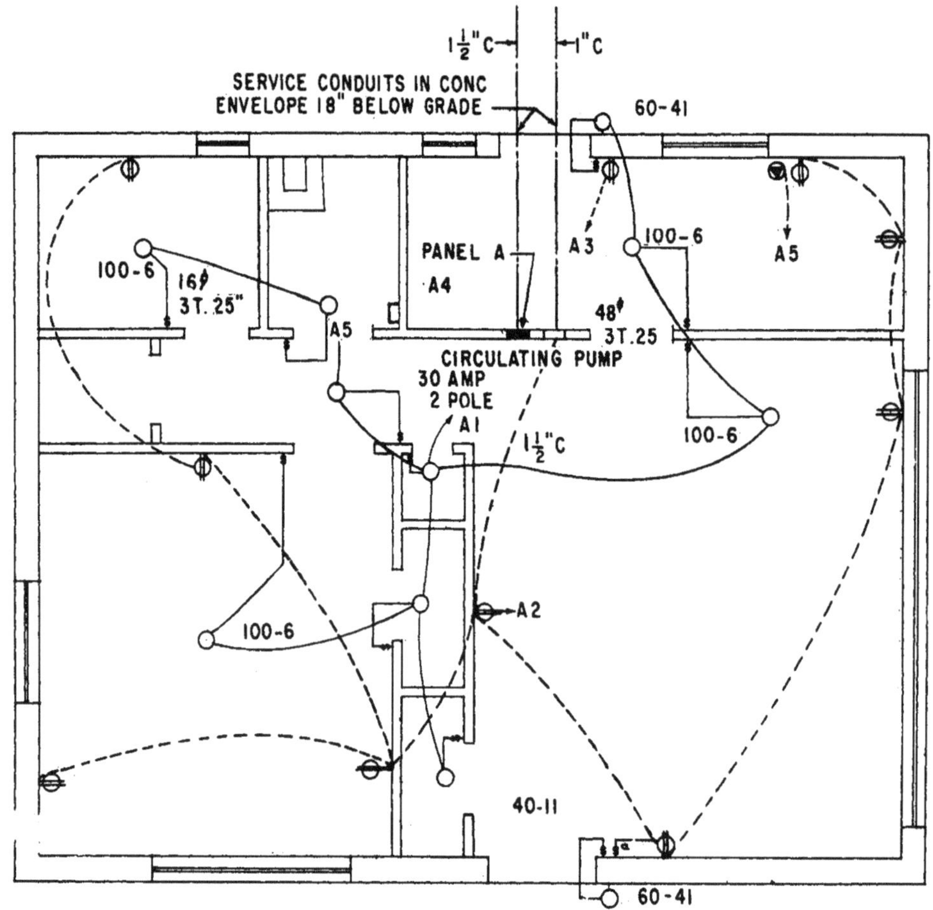

Figure 8.—Electrical plan.

2.—EARTHWORK 3.—CONCRETE 4.—MASONRY 5.—MISCELLANEOUS STEEL AND IRON 6.—CARPENTRY AND JOINERY 7.—LATHING AND PLASTERING 8.—TILE WORK 9.—FINISH FLOORING 10.—GLAZING 11.—FINISHING HARDWARE 12.—PLUMBING 13.—HEATING 14.—ELECTRICAL WORK 15.—FIELD PAINTING.

A section under "Specific Conditions" usually begins with a subsection of GENERAL REQUIREMENTS which apply to the phase of construction being considered. Under Section 6, CARPENTRY AND JOINERY, for example, the first section might go as follows:

6-01. GENERAL REQUIREMENTS. All framing, rough carpentry, and finishing woodwork required for the proper completion of the building shall be provided. All woodwork shall be protected from the weather, and the building shall be thoroughly dry before the finish is placed. All finish shall be dressed, smoothed, and sandpapered at the mill, and in addition shall be hand smoothed and sandpapered at the building where necessary to produce proper finish. Nailing shall be done, as far as practicable, in concealed places, and all nails in finishing work shall be set. All lumber shall be S4S (meaning, "surfaced on 4 sides"); all materials for millwork and finish shall be kiln-dried; all rough and framing lumber shall be air- or kiln-dried. Any cutting, fitting, framing, and blocking necessary for the accommodation of other work shall be provided. All nails, spikes, screws, bolts, plates, clips, and other fastenings and rough hardware necessary for the proper completion of the building shall be provided.

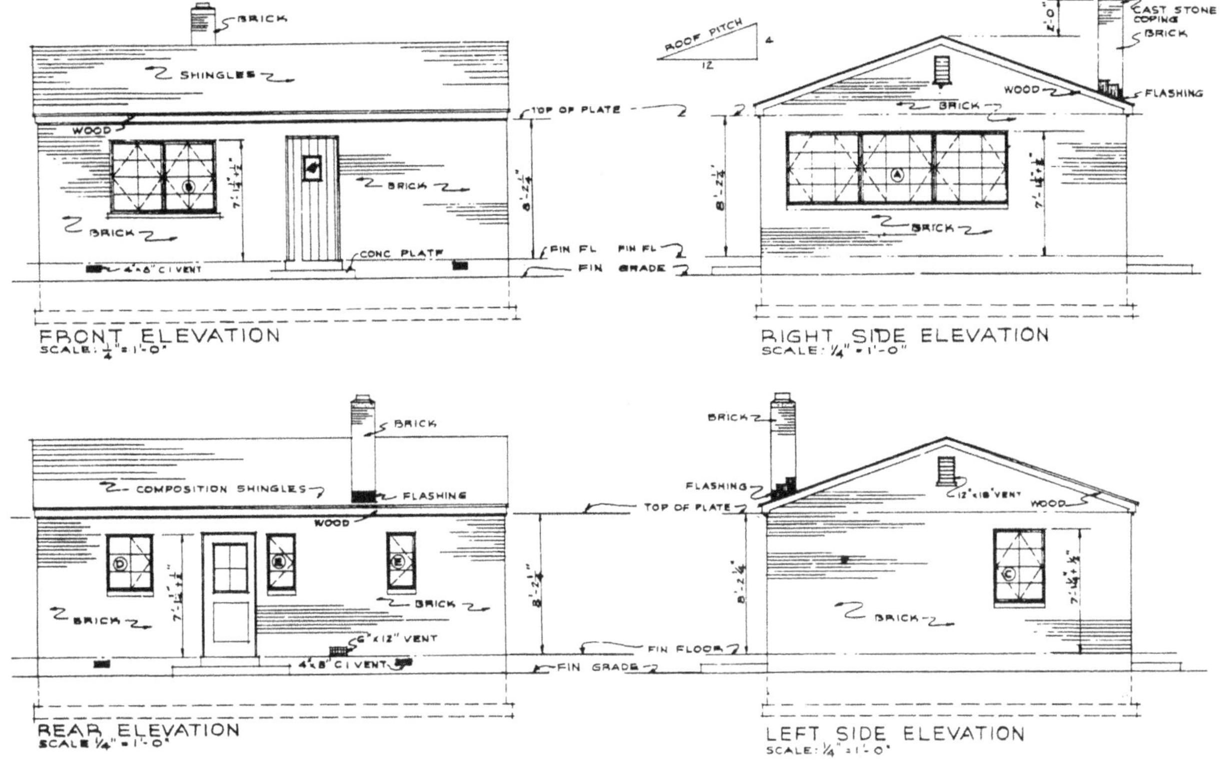

Figure 2-9.—Elevations.

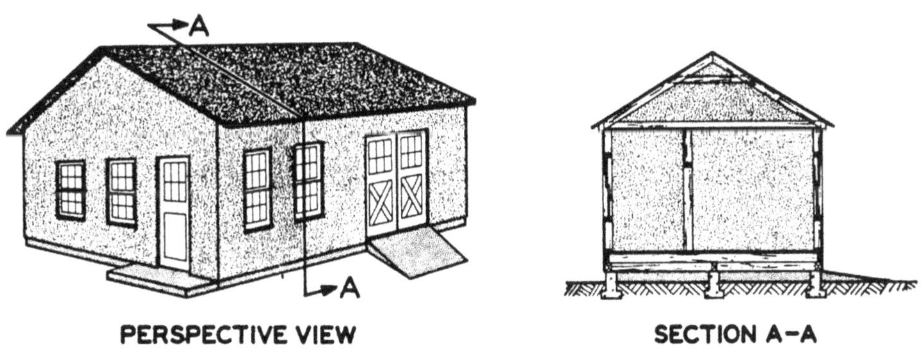

TYPICAL SMALL BUILDING SHOWING CUTTING PLANE A-A AND SECTION DEVELOPED FROM THE CUTTING PLANE

Figure 10.—Development of a section view.

All finishing hardware shall be installed in accordance with the manufacturers' directions. Calking and flashing shall be provided where indicated, or where necessary to provide weathertight construction.

Next after the General Requirements for Carpentry and Joinery, there is generally a subsection on "Grading," in which the kinds and grades of the various woods to be used in the structure are specified. Subsequent subsections

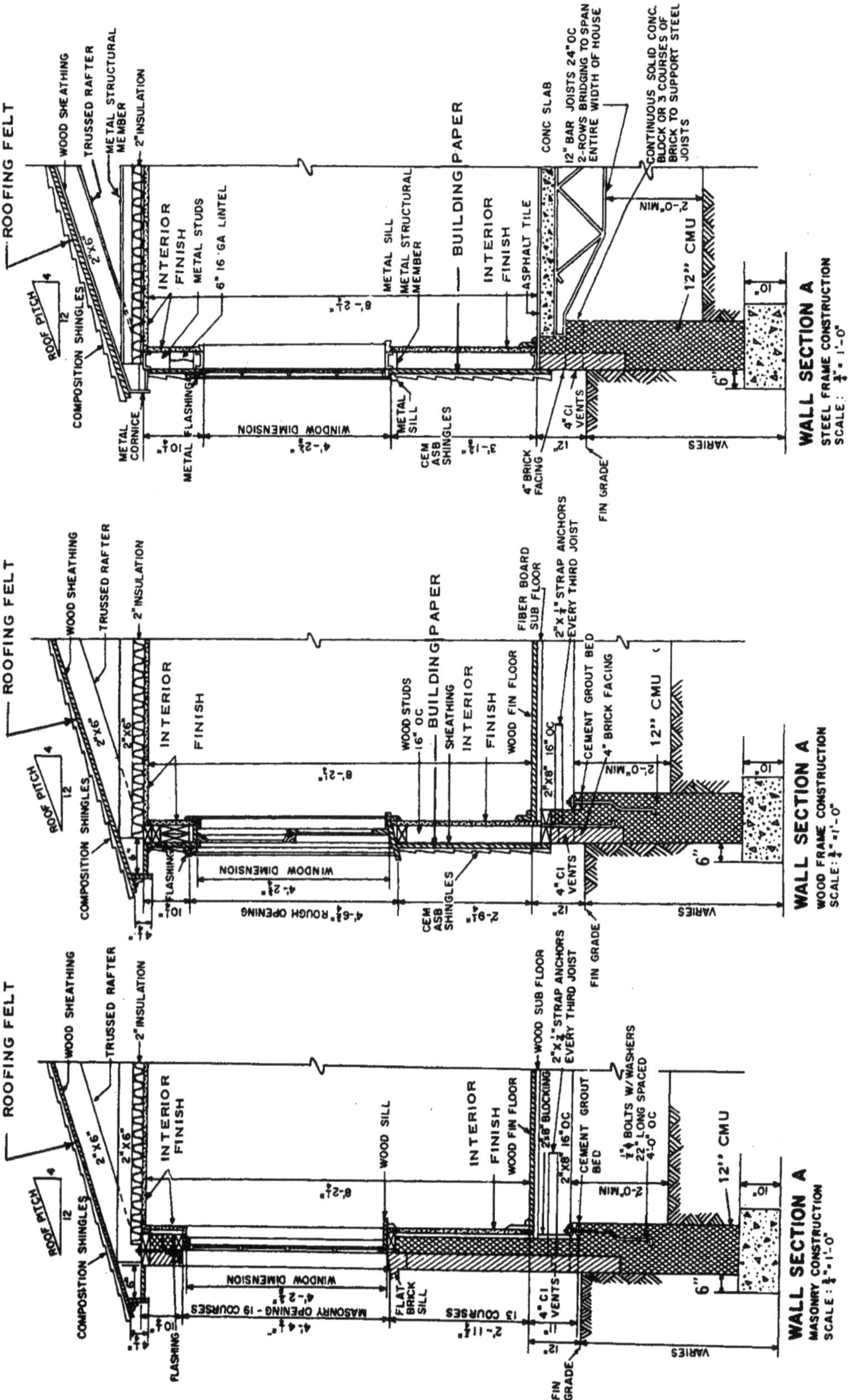

Figure 11.—Wall sections

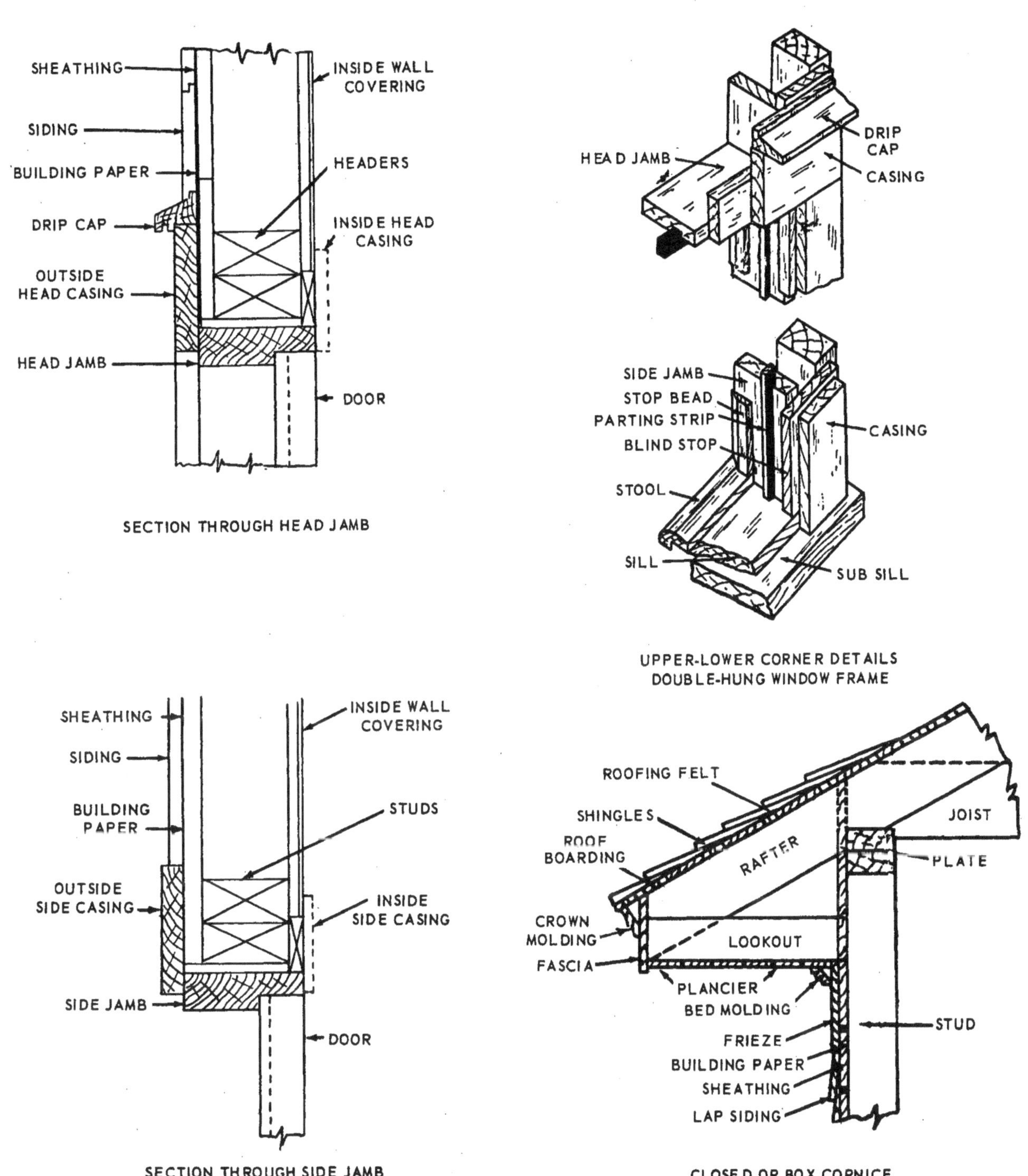

Figure 12.—Door, window and eave details.

specify various quality criteria and standards of workmanship for the various aspects of the rough and finish carpentry work, under such headings as FRAMING; SILLS, PLATES, AND GIRDERS; FLOOR JOISTS AND ROOF RAFTERS; STUDDING; and so on. An example of one of these subsections follows:

STUDDING for walls and partitions shall have doubled plates and doubled stud caps. Studs shall be set plumb and not to exceed 16-in. centers and in true alignment; they shall be bridged with one row of 2 x 4 pieces, set flatwise, fitted tightly, and nailed securely to each stud. Studding shall be doubled around openings and the heads of openings shall rest on the inner studs. Openings in partitions having widths of 4 ft and over shall be trussed. In wood frame construction, studs shall be trebled at corners to form posts.

From the above samples, you can see that a knowledge of the relevant specifications is as essential to the construction supervisor and the construction artisan as a knowledge of the construction drawings.

It is very important that the proper spec be used to cover the material requested. In cases in which the material is not covered by a Government spec, the ASTM (American Society for Testing Materials) spec or some other approved commercial spec may be used. It is EXTREMELY IMPORTANT in using specifications to cite all amendments, including the latest changes.

As a rule, the specs are provided for each project by the A/E (ARCHITECT-ENGINEERS). These are the OFFICIAL guidelines approved by the chief engineer or his representative for use during construction. These requirements should NOT be deviated from without prior approval from proper authority. This approval is usually obtained by means of a change order. When there is disagreement between the specifications and drawings, the specifications should normally be followed; however, check with higher authority in each case.

IV. BUILDER'S MATHEMATICS

The Builder has many occasions for the employment of the processes of ordinary arithmetic, and he must be thoroughly familiar with the methods of determining the areas and volumes of the various plane and solid geometrical figures. Only a few practical applications and a few practical suggestions, will be given here.

RATIO AND PROPORTION

There are a great many practical applications of ratio and proportion in the construction field. A few examples are as follows:

Some dimensions on construction drawings (such as, for example, distances from base lines and elevations of surfaces) are given in ENGINEER'S instead of CARPENTER's measure. Engineer's measure is measure in feet and decimal parts of a foot, or in inches and decimal parts of an inch, such as 100.15 ft or 11.14 in. Carpenter's measure is measure in yards, feet, inches, and even-denominator fractions of an inch, such as 1/2 in., 1/4 in., 1/16 in., 1/32 in., and 1/64 in.

You must know how to convert an engineer's measure given on a construction drawing to a carpenter's measure. Besides this, it will often happen that calculations you make yourself may produce a result in feet and decimal parts of a foot, which result you will have to convert to carpenter's measure. To convert engineer's to carpenter's measure you can use ratio and proportion as follows:

Let's say that you want to convert 100.14 ft to feet and inches to the nearest 1/16 in. The 100 you don't need to convert, since it is already in feet. What you need to do, first, is to find out how many twelfths of a foot (that is, how many inches) there are in 14/100 ft. Set this up as a proportional equation as follows: x:12::14:100.

You know that in a proportional equation the product of the means equals the product of the extremes. Consequently, 100x = (12 x 14), or 168. Then x = 168/100, or 1.68 in. Next question is, how many 16ths of an in. are there in 68/100 in.? Set this up, too, as a proportional equation, thus: x:16::68:100. Then 100x = 1088, and x = 10 88/100 sixteenths. Since 88/100 of a sixteenth is more than one-half of a sixteenth, you ROUND OFF by calling it 11/16. In 100.14 ft, then, there are 100 ft 1 11/16 in. For example:

A.

$$\underbrace{x:\overset{\text{means}}{12::14}:100}_{\text{Extremes}}$$

Product of extremes = product of means:

$$100\ x = 168$$
$$x = 1.68 \text{ IN.}$$

B. x:16::68:100

$$100\ x = 1088$$

$$x = 10.88$$

$$x = 10\ \frac{88}{100} \text{ sixteenths}$$

Rounded off to 11/16

Another way to convert engineer's measurements to carpenter's measurements is to multiply the decimal portion of a foot by 12 to get inches; multiply the decimal by 16 to get the fraction of an inch.

There are many other practical applications of ratio and proportion in the construction field. Suppose, for example, that a table tells you that, for the size and type of brick wall you happen to be laying, 12,321 bricks and 195 cu ft of mortar are required per every 1000 sq ft of wall. How many bricks and how much mortar will be needed for 750 sq ft of the same wall? You simply set up equations as follows; for example:

Brick: x:750::12,321:1000
Mortar: x:750::195:1000

Brick: $\frac{X}{750} = \frac{12{,}321}{1000}$ Cross multiply

$1000\ X = 9{,}240{,}750$ Divide
$X = 9{,}240.75 = 9241$ Brick.

Mortar: $\frac{X}{750} = \frac{195}{1000}$. Cross multiply

$1000\ X = 146{,}250$ Divide
$X = 146.25 = 146\ 1/4$ cu ft

Suppose, for another example, that the ingredient proportions by volume for the type of concrete you are making are 1 cu ft cement to 1.7 cu ft sand to 2.8 cu ft coarse aggregate. Suppose you know as well, by reference to a table, that ingredients combined in the amounts indicated will produce 4.07 cu ft of concrete. How much of each ingredient will be required to make a cu yd of concrete?

Remember here, first, that there are not 9, but 27 (3 ft x 3 ft x 3 ft) cu ft in a cu yd. Your proportional equations will be as follows:

Cement: x:27::1:4.07

Sand: x:27::1.7:4.07

Coarse aggregate: x:27::2.8:4.07

Cement: x:27::1:4.07

$$\frac{x}{27} = \frac{1}{4.07}$$

$$4.07\ x = 27$$

$$x = 6.63 \text{ cu ft Cement}$$

Sand: x:27::1.7:4.07

$$\frac{x}{27} = \frac{1.7}{4.07}$$

$$4.07\ x = 45.9$$

$$x = 11.28 \text{ cu ft Sand}$$

Coarse aggregate: x:27::2.8:407

$$\frac{x}{27} = \frac{2.8}{4.07}$$

$$4.07\ x = 75.6$$

$$x = 18.57 \text{ cu ft Coarse aggregate}$$

ARITHMETICAL OPERATIONS

The formulas for finding the area and volume of geometric figures are expressed in algebraic equations which are called formulas. A few of the more important formulas and their mathematical solutions will be discussed in this section.

To get an area, you multiply 2 linear measures together, and to get a volume you multiply 3 linear measures together. The linear measures you multiply together must all be expressed in the SAME UNITS; you cannot, for example, multiply a length in feet by a width in inches to get a result in square feet or in square inches.

Dimensions of a feature on a construction drawing are not always given in the same units. For a concrete wall, for example, the length and height are usually given in feet and the thickness in inches. Furthermore, you may want to get a result in units which are different from any shown on the drawing. Concrete volume, for example, is usually expressed in cubic yards, while the dimensions of concrete work are given on the drawings in feet and inches.

You can save yourself a good many steps in calculating by using fractions to convert the original dimension units into the desired end-result units. Take 1 in., for example. To express 1 in. in feet, you simply put it over 12, thus: 1/12 ft. To express 1 in. in yards, you simply put it over 36, thus: 1/36 yd. In the same manner, to express 1 ft in yards you simply put it over 3, thus 1/3 yd.

Suppose now that you want to calculate the number of cu yd of concrete in a wall 32 ft long by 14 ft high by 8 in. thick. You can express all these in yards and set up your problem thus:

$$\frac{32}{3} \times \frac{14}{3} \times \frac{8}{36}$$

Next you can cancel out, thus:

$$\frac{\overset{16}{\cancel{32}}}{3} \times \frac{\cancel{14}}{3} \times \frac{8}{\underset{\underset{9}{\cancel{18}}}{\cancel{36}}} = \frac{896}{81}$$

Dividing 896 by 81, you get 11.06 cu yds of concrete in the wall.

The right triangle is a triangle which contains one right (90°) angle. The following letters will denote the parts of the triangle indicated in figure 2-13—a = altitude, b = base, c = hypotenuse.

In solving a right triangle, the length of any side may be found if the lengths of the other two sides are given. The combinations of 3-4-5 (lengths of sides) or any multiple of these combinations will come out to a whole number. The following examples show the formula for finding each side. Each of these formulas is derived from the master formula $c^2 = a^2 + b^2$.

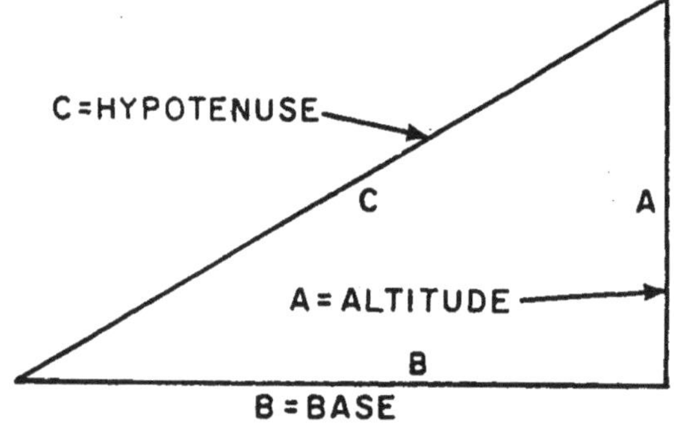

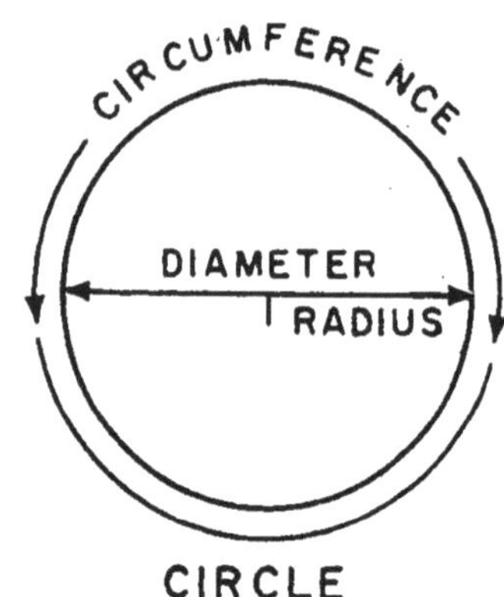

Figure 13.—Right triangle and circle.

(1) Find c when a = 3, and b = 4.

$$c = \sqrt{a^2 + b^2} = \sqrt{3^2 + 4^2} = \sqrt{9 + 16} = \sqrt{25} = 5$$

(2) Find a when b = 8, and c = 10.

$$a = \sqrt{c^2 - b^2} = \sqrt{10^2 - 8^2} = \sqrt{100 - 64} = \sqrt{36} = 6$$

(3) Find b when a = 9, and c = 15.

$$b = \sqrt{c^2 - a^2} = \sqrt{15^2 - 9^2} = \sqrt{225 - 81} = \sqrt{144} = 12.$$

There are tables from which the square roots of numbers may be found; otherwise, they may be found arithmetically as explained later in this chapter.

Areas And Volumes Of Geometric Figures

This section on areas and volumes of geometric figures will be limited to the most commonly used geometric figures. Reference books, such as Mathematics, Vol. 1, are available for additional information if needed. Areas are expressed in square units and volumes in cubic units.

1. A circle is a plane figure bounded by a curved line every point of which is the same distance from the center.
   a. The curved line is called the circumference.
   b. A straight line drawn from the center to any point on the circumference is called a radius. (r = 1/2 the diameter.)
   c. A straight line drawn from one point of the circumference through the center and terminating on the opposite point of the circumference is called a diameter. (d = 2 times the radius.) See figure 2-13.
   d. The area of a circle is found by the following formulas: $A = \pi r^2$ or $A = .7854\ d^2$. (π is pronounced pie = 3.1416 or 3 1/7, .7854 is 1/4 of π.) Example: Find the area of a circle whose radius is 7". $A = \pi r^2 = 3\ 1/7 \times 7^2 = 22/7 \times 49 = 154$ sq in. If you use the second formula you obtain the same results.
   e. The circumference of a circle is found by multiplying π times the diameter or 2 times π times the radius. Example: Find the circumference of a circle whose diameter is 56 inches. $C = \pi d = 3.1415 \times 56 = 175.9296$ inches.

2. The area of a right triangle is equal to one-half the product of the base by the altitude. (Area = 1/2 base x altitude.) Example: Find the area of a triangle whose base is 16" and altitude 6". Solution:

$$A = 1/2\ bh = 1/2 \times 16 \times 6 = 48 \text{ sq in.}$$

3. The volume of a cylinder is found by multiplying the area of the base times the height. ($V = 3.1416 \times r^2 \times h$). Example: Find the volume of a cylinder which has a radius of 8 in. and a height of 4 ft. Solution:

$$8 \text{ in} = \frac{2}{3} \text{ ft and } \left(\frac{2}{3}\right) 2 = \frac{4}{9} \text{ sq ft.}$$

$$V = 3.1416 \times \frac{4}{9} \times 4 = \frac{50.2656}{9} = 5.59 \text{ cu ft.}$$

4. The volume of a rectangular solid equals the length x width x height. (V = lwh.) Example: Find the volume of a rectangular solid which has a length of 6 ft, a width of 3 ft, and a height of 2 ft. Solution:

$$V = lwh = 6 \times 3 \times 2 = 36 \text{ cu ft.}$$

5. The volume of a cone may be found by multiplying one-third times the area of the base times the height.

$$\left(V = \frac{1}{3} \pi r^2 h\right)$$

Example: Find the volume of a cone when the radius of its base is 2 ft and its height is 9 ft. Solution:

$$\pi = 3.1416,\ r = 2,\ 2^2 = 4$$

$$V = \frac{1}{3} r^2 h = \frac{1}{3} \times 3.1416 \times 4 \times 9 = 37.70 \text{ cu ft.}$$

Powers And Roots

1. Powers—When we multiply several numbers together, as 2 x 3 x 4 = 24, the numbers 2, 3, and 4 are factors and 24 the product. The operation of raising a number to a power is a special case of multiplication in which the factors are all equal. The power of a number is the number of times the number itself is to be taken as a factor. Example: 2^4 is 16. The second power is called the square of the number, as 3^2. The third power of a number is called the cube of the number, as 5^3. The exponent of a number is a number placed to the right and above a base to show how many times the base is used as a factor. Example:

4^3 ← exponent = ← base

$$4 \times 4 \times 4 = 64.$$

2. Roots—To indicate a root, use the sign $\sqrt{\ }$, which is called the radical sign. A small figure, called the index of the root, is placed in the opening of the sign to show which root is to be taken. The square root of a number is one of the two equal factors into which a number is

divided. Example: $\sqrt{81} = \sqrt{9 \times 9} = 9$. The cube root is one of the three equal factors into which a number is divided. Example: $\sqrt[3]{125} = \sqrt[3]{5 \times 5 \times 5} = 5$.

Square Root

1. The square root of any number is that number which, when multiplied by itself, will produce the first number. For example; the square root of 121 is 11 because 11 times 11 equals 121.

2. How to extract the square root arithmetically:

```
                 95.
  √9025     √90'25.

           : -81

     180 :   925
      +5 :  -925

     185 :   000
```

a. Begin at the decimal point and divide the given number into groups of 2 digits each (as far as possible), going from right to left and/or left to right.
b. Find the greatest number (9) whose square is contained in the first or left hand group (90). Square this number (9) and place it under the first pair of digits (90), then subtract.
c. Bring down the next pair of digits (25) and add it to the remainder (9).
d. Multiply the first digit in the root by 20 and use it as a trial divisor (180). This trial divisor (180) will go into the new dividend (925) five times. This number, 5 (second digit in the root), is added back to the trial divisor, obtaining the true divisor (185).
e. The true divisor (185) is multiplied by the second digit (5) and placed under the remainder (925). Subtract and the problem is solved.
f. If there is still a remainder and you want to carry the problem further, add zeros (in pairs) and continue the above process.

Coverage Calculations

You will frequently have occasion to estimate the number of linear feet of boards of a given size, or the number of tiles, asbestos shingles, and the like, required to cover a given area. Let's take the matter of linear feet of boards first.

What you do here is calculate, first, the number of linear feet of board required to cover 1 sq ft. For boards laid edge-to-edge, you base your calculations on the total width of a board. For boards which will lap each other, you base your calculations on the width laid TO THE WEATHER, meaning the total width minus the width of the lap.

Since there are 144 sq in. in a sq ft, linear footage to cover a given area can be calculated as follows. Suppose your boards are to be laid 8 in. to the weather. If you divide 8 in. into 144 sq in., the result (which is 18 in., or 1.5 ft) will be the linear footage required to cover a sq ft. If you have, say, 100 sq ft to cover, the linear footage required will be 100 x 1.5, or 150 ft.

To estimate the number of tiles, asbestos shingles, and the like required to cover a given area, you first calculate the number of units required to cover a sq ft. Suppose, for example, you are dealing with 9 in. x 9 in. asphalt tiles. The area of one of these is 9 in. x 9 in. or 81 sq in. In a sq ft there are 144 sq in. If it takes 1 to cover 81 sq in., how many will it take to cover 144 sq in.? Just set up a proportional equation, as follows.

$$1:81::x:144$$

When you work this out, you will find that it takes 1.77 tiles to cover a sq ft. To find the number of tiles required to cover 100 sq ft, simply multiply by 100. How do you multiply anything by 100? Just move the decimal point 2 places to the right. Consequently, it takes 177 9 x 9 asphalt tiles to cover 100 sq ft of area.

Board Measure

BOARD MEASURE is a method of measuring lumber in which the basic unit is an abstract volume 1 ft long by 1 ft wide by 1 in. thick. This abstract volume or unit is called a BOARD FOOT.

There are several formulas for calculating the number of board feet in a piece of given dimensions. Since lumber dimensions are most frequently indicated by width and thickness in inches and length in feet, the following formula is probably the most practical.

$$\frac{\text{Thickness in in. x width in in. x length in ft}}{12}$$

= board feet

Suppose you are calculating the number of board feet in a 14-ft length of 2 x 4. Applying the formula, you get:

$$\frac{\overset{1}{\cancel{2}} \times \overset{2}{\cancel{4}} \times 14}{\underset{\underset{3}{\cancel{6}}}{\cancel{12}}} = \frac{28}{3} = 9\ 1/3 \text{ bd ft}$$

The chief practical use of board measure is in cost calculations, since lumber is bought and sold by the board foot. Any lumber less than 1 in. thick is presumed to be 1 in. thick for board measure purposes. Board measure is calculated on the basis of the NOMINAL, not the ACTUAL, dimensions of lumber.

The actual size of a piece of dimension lumber (such as a 2 x 4, for example) is usually less than the nominal size.

CPSIA information can be obtained
at www.ICGtesting.com
Printed in the USA
LVHW062159150122
708690LV00020B/207